Modular Programming in COBOL
Russell M. Armstrong

Functional Analysis of Information Networks
Hal B. Becker

Functional Analysis of Information Processing
Grayce M. Booth

Effective Use of ANS COBOL Computer Programming Language
Laurence S. Cohn

The Database Administrator
John K. Lyon

Software Reliability: Principles and Practices
Glenford J. Myers

The Psychology of Business Systems
William C. Ramsgard

The Art of Software Testing
Glenford J. Myers

Data Base Design and Performance: A Case Study Approach
S. Atre

An Introduction to Software Quality Control
Chin-Kuei Cho

Build Program Technique: A Practical Approach for the Development of Automatic Software Generation Systems
John G. Rice

Motivating and Managing Computer Personnel
J. Daniel Couger, Robert A. Zawacki

MOTIVATING AND MANAGING COMPUTER PERSONNEL

MOTIVATING AND MANAGING COMPUTER PERSONNEL

J. Daniel Couger
Professor of Computer and Management Science
University of Colorado

Robert A. Zawacki
Professor of Management and Organization
University of Colorado

A WILEY-INTERSCIENCE PUBLICATION
JOHN WILEY & SONS • New York • Chichester • Brisbane • Toronto

This publication is designed to provide accurate and authoritative information in regard to the subject matter covered. It is sold with the understanding that the publisher is not engaged in rendering legal, accounting, or other professional service. If legal advice or other expert assistance is required, the services of a competent professional person should be sought. *From a Declaration of Principles jointly adopted by a Committee of the American Bar Association and a Committee of Publishers.*

Library of Congress Cataloging in Publication Data:

Couger, J Daniel.
    Motivating and managing computer personnel.

    "A Wiley-Interscience publication."
    Includes index.
    1. Electric data processing departments—Personnel management. 2. Employee motivation. I. Zawacki, Robert A., joint author. II. Title.

HF5548.2.C69   658'.054'0683   80-19925
ISBN 0-471-08485-9

Printed in the United States of America

10 9 8 7 6 5 4 3 2 1

From Dan Couger
To my wife's mother,
Ethel Thomas

From Bob Zawacki
To my parents,
Mr. and Mrs. Mike Zawacki

ACKNOWLEDGMENTS

We wish to acknowledge the assistance of a number of people in the preparation of this book. Our first recognition must be given to J. Richard Hackman and Greg R. Oldham, the developers of the Job Diagnostic Survey, and William E. Rosenbach, who modified the JDS to include data on goalsetting and feedback. They proved the validity and reliability of the survey instrument. Our version, the JDS/DP, preserves the integrity of the instrument and expands it to include questions specific to the computer field.

Next we wish to recognize the contribution of Edward B. Oppermann in assisting in the statistical analysis of the survey data. John E. Dittrich and Charles L. Hinkle developed most of the cases in the appendix. Our excellent typists were Kathy Abeyta, Ellyn Munroe, Anne Reints, Dennis Atkinson, and Jo Anne Copeland.

Finally, to those thousands of individuals who participated in the survey (who didn't throw away the survey form!), we are particularly grateful. We hope the establishment of national norms justifies their time on completing the survey and that the analysis of survey results will be helpful both to the survey respondents and to all persons in the computer field.

J. DANIEL COUGER
ROBERT A. ZAWACKI

Colorado Springs, Colorado
August 1980

CONTENTS

FIGURES

TABLES

MOTIVATING AND MANAGING
COMPUTER PERSONNEL

1

INTRODUCTION

This book is designed for managers of data processing and for persons aspiring to management positions. Much of it is also useful for nonmanagerial personnel, since it should encourage all readers to be introspective about personal attitudes and objectives. Understanding one's self is important for any employee—supervisor or nonsupervisor.

The book provides norms against which a person can evaluate his or her job. This self-evaluation process will lead to a clearer understanding on one's job environment. The process will help to ensure that the kinds of satisfaction expected from the job actually accrue. Further, a procedure is provided to help data processing (DP) managers redesign any jobs in their departments that lack the dimension necessary to promote employee satisfaction and productivity.

Need for Increasing Motivation

In a 1980 speech in Chicago, George Gallup reported the results of a survey of the U.S. work force. He disclosed an

1

alarming statistic on productivity. Four of ten workers in the survey responded that they could increase productivity as much as 30 percent; six of ten responded that they could increase productivity as much as 20 percent.

What motivates employees to produce to their capacity? Motivational research has produced some solid answers to that question and the Gallup poll will undoubtedly create interest in such research results. However, until recently this research was not directly applicable to the computer field. Our research, however, has concentrated on the computer field. We began with a nationwide survey on motivation of analysts, programmers, and operations personnel. The survey revealed some characteristics unique to this field. The survey results were reported at the 1979 and 1980 National Computer Conference and in a series of three articles in *Datamation*.

We recently completed a nationwide survey of DP managers at three levels in the management hierarchy. Comparing these results to survey results of general (non-DP) managers identified some significant differences. The goal of this book is to show how a manager and a subordinate can deal with these differences to produce a work environment that motivates workers. First we examine some of the problems that have highlighted the need for improved productivity.

Expanding Backlog of Work

The expanding backlog for new system development is a cause for concern in the typical DP department. The inability to reduce the backlog is a result of five major factors:

1 *Increasing complexity of systems*   Despite the continuous introduction of improved analysis and program-

ming techniques, personnel productivity has not kept pace with the demand for new systems. Personnel costs occupy a significantly higher proportion of the DP budget each year. In 1970 they were only 30 percent of the total budget. Five years later the proportion was at 40 percent. In 1980 personnel costs amounted to over 50 percent of the total DP budget. The increasing cost is caused by (1) the diminishing cost of hardware (e.g., the price/performance ratio of today's equipment is four times that of five years ago) and (2) the increasing complexity of applications. In earlier years, companies concentrated on computerizing administrative systems. Today they are concentrating on lifestream applications—those key to the life and growth of the firm. Not only are those systems more complex, but more design time is require to ensure their reliability. The company could work around an accounting or a personnel system that was temporarily down, but when the system is at the heart of the company's operations, down time is prohibitively expensive. More effort and time are required in the design of these systems. Obviously, another reason for the rise in personnel cost is inflation. Labor costs have been affected by inflation more than have hardware costs.

2 *Increasing quantity of systems* As users continue to learn more about computing and information systems, they increase their volume of system requests.

3 *Turnover* Job hopping has reached epidemic proportions. A recent *Datamation* survey showed the national turnover rate to be 28 percent overall and 34 percent for application programmers. The learning curve for new employees reduces productivity significantly.

4 *Increasing maintenance cost* The problem of backlog of new systems is intensified by the declining percentage of the budget spent on new system development.

Maintenance activities now consume over 50 percent of the budget for programming and analysis in most companies. In some companies maintenance accounts for more than 75 percent of the total systems personnel budget.

5 *Shortage of qualified personnel*   Recruitment has become a major issue. No longer just a personnel department concern, it is increasingly a drain on the time and energy of management. The situation has become so bad that an East Coast firm recently offered an ounce of gold as an inducement to employment. Or, if preferred, the potential employee could choose the alternative of a free trip for two to the Bahamas. The prospects for reducing the shortage are not good. University output will not catch up with demand any time in the near future. Independent training organizations or vendor training groups are equally unlikely to fill the gap. Training will continue to consume a large share of each company's budget and will drain resources from system development in order to teach courses.

Major Issues

This book attacks some problems that are obvious to almost everyone in the profession—the turnover problem, for example. It also deals with issues that are not so apparent, like the issue of whether job satisfaction leads to productivity or whether the two are mutually exclusive.

The view that high salary and fringe benefits are the solution to the turnover problem is calamitous. Companies that concentrate solely on financial inducements will be disappointed in the results. The job itself is the major motivator, as shown in Chapter 2 using data from several surveys. Surprisingly, improving motivation through concentrating on the job itself is not a huge undertaking in either time or resources. The scope of that task is small compared with that of recruitment. Managers can make major improvements on a job's motivating potential in a relatively short period of time, using the procedures explained in this book.

People Problems Common to All Organizations

Rankings of problems that concern managers place people problems at the top in almost every industry. This is not a recent phenomenon. Surveys in the 1960s and 1970s revealed the same situations. However, several industries have unique problems. The computer industry has some unique problems deriving from the technology and others caused by the unique characteristics of computer personnel.

Our survey revealed two characteristics of computer personnel that require special management action—their low social need and their high growth need. In addition, the scarcity of qualified personnel necessitates special care in managing computer personnel: they will be more vocal about their feelings because the risk of retribution is low, and they will not be very patient about promised changes. DP managers must be more responsive to employee requests and needs than their managerial comterparts in other parts of the company. A dissatisfied DP employee can find employment elsewhere almost overnight.

Profession Rather than Company Loyalty

For some time there has been a feeling by managers that DP personnel have more loyalty to their profession than to their company. For example, a college graduate in the marketing department appears to more easily align career objectives with the company promotion path. In banking, for example, a new college graduate with a financial management degree is more content to choose the company promotion channels than to job hop. The programmer or analyst appears to use persons in the profession rather than persons in the company as his or her reference point for financial and job equity. This is a problem that can be reduced, although not eliminated, as discussed in Chapters 3 and 5.

National Norms for Computer Personnel

Some points need to be made about the strengths and weaknesses of this book. The principal strengths are the data base and rigorous statistical analysis of those data. This is the first national data base containing computer personnel perceptions about their jobs. The careful design of the survey instrument, the Job Diagnostic Survey for Data Processing (JDS/DP), and the sampling approach ensure the validity of the data base. Equal rigor was used in the selection of statistical techniques for data analysis. Therefore, the explanation of attitudes and perceptions of computer personnel is based on solid analytic approaches rather than the authors' opinions.

Through this approach we were able to establish national norms against which managers could compare their own employees (Chapters 2 to 4). This result is the most important contribution of the book, in our view. With these benchmarks, management has a way to measure employee motivation and to pinpoint problems.

The second principal strength of the book is identification of ways to improve motivation. After the review of motivation theory, specific procedures for job evaluation and work redesign are provided (Chapters 3 and 5). For companies where the motivational environment evidences few problems, the same procedure can be used to "fine tune" jobs. Examples are provided in Chapter 4.

The third strength of the book is in the section on matching employee characteristics to the appropriate task. The national norms are means (averages). Chapter 7 discusses how to match task assignments to personnel whose characteristics deviate from the norms. An example is the identification of the type of employee who is best suited for work on maintaining systems instead of developing new systems. After classifying programmer and analyst tasks into four major categories, we identify the type of management style best suited to motivate employees in each of the four categories. The analysis includes all jobs within the DP department, not just the jobs in the development area.

The theories of motivation are carefully analyzed, but the principal thrust of the book is on application of the theories. Alternative practices that enhance motivation are discussed in detail, and the ways these changes increase productivity are identified. Examples are provided from a number of implementations in industry and government.

Speculative Areas

Data from our national surveys identify a number of areas of concern. Most of these problems dictate an obvious course of action, e.g., the problem of lack of feedback as perceived by every job category in the DP department.

The *cause* of other problems is not nearly so clear. The principal weakness of the research is in identifying causes of the unique differences of personnel in the computer profession Causes cannot be deduced from the survey data with 100 percent assurance. Low need for social interaction, compared to other professions, is clearly identified by the JDS/DP. The reason the DP profession has such low social need is not clear. Do we attract into the profession personnel with low social need, or is there something about the job that produces this characteristic? Here we must speculate. However, we do not depend solely on a "guess." We have some educated guesses, supported by detailed analysis (Chapter 7).

Several areas require speculation at this stage of our research. However, we are designing additional survey instruments to ferret out data to explain more of the causes for problems perceived by our profession. That information will be the subject of the next book in this series of books on motivating and managing DP personnel.

2

ANALYSIS OF KEY FACTORS FOR MOTIVATION OF DATA PROCESSING PROFESSIONALS

Now more than twenty-five years old, the computer profession may be assuming some of the behavioral problems characteristic of older disciplines such as engineering and accounting.

According to *Work in America,*[1] worker alienation is one of the major problems in organizations today. The report indicates that the job itself has not kept pace with the changes in our society such as worker attitudes, aspirations, and values.

Managers have attempted to reduce worker alienation and improve the quality of work life by trying out a plethora of approaches for the humanization of work. Some past and current attempts include sensitivity training, management by objectives, shortening of the workweek, and greater worker involvement in the decision-making process.

Signs of job dissatisfaction are also emerging in the computer field. Although the aura of excitement of a dynamic field continues to attract persons into the profession, it no longer retains them. Individuals are seeking a more meaningful experience than just being a part of a fast-growing profession. The job itself must produce the essential elements of satisfaction—the peripheral benefits of being at the forefront of technology are important but alone are insufficient to keep a person motivated.

The behavioralists have identified factors key to motivation and satisfaction in other disciplines. But are they the same for the computer profession? Even if they are identical, does each factor have the same degree of importance for DP professionals?

Profile of the Organizations Surveyed

The nongovernment organizations surveyed represented the following industries: food processing, airlines, electronics, retailing, banking, insurance, and mail order. Their DP organizations ranged in size from 25 to 150 employees and represented all geographic regions of the United States.

The governmental organizations were located in 15 states. Their DP organizations varied in size from 30 to 200 employees.

Over 1000 DP professionals (analysts, programmer/ analysts, and programmers) were surveyed. More than 1500 personnel in other DP jobs were surveyed.

Scope of the Survey

This chapter contains only the results of the survey of DP professionals: analysts, programmer/analysts, and programmers. Survey results for all other DP jobs, including supervision, are reported in Chapters 3 and 4.

Selection of the Survey Instrument

We originally sought to design a survey instrument peculiar to the computer field. After two months of evaluating various instruments we decided to utilize, instead, the Job Diagnostic Survey (JDS) developed by J. Richard Hackman (University of Illinois) and Greg R. Oldham (Yale University), for two principal reasons:

1 The JDS is conceptually sound. Its validity and reliability have been substantiated[2] in studies of more than 6000 subjects on more than 500 different jobs in more than 50 different organizations.

2 A major objective is to compare our results with prior studies of personnel in other professions. Our hypothesis on the difference between DP professionals and other personnel could be tested.

We expanded the survey questionnaire to include other elements: employee perceptions on relative importance of problems relating to maintenance, realistic work schedules, access to the computer, access to supervisors, and access to others (e.g., users or personnel in other departments whose work affected their own). Also added to the survey instrument were sections on objective setting and the relative importance of eight categories of compensation. This modified instrument is called the JDS/DP.

*The Hackman/Oldham JDS is an extended and refined version of the Hackman/Lawler questionnaire that has undergone three major revisions. For further information see J. R. Hackman and E. E. Lawler III, "Employee Reactions to Job Characteristics," *Journal of Applied Psychology Monograph,* Vol. 55 (1971), pp. 259–286.

All survey results were analyzed by the computer packages for Analysis of Variance (ANOVA) and Statistical Processing for the Social Sciences (SPSS).

Core Job Dimensions and Critical Psychological States

The Hackman/Oldham (H/O) model (Figure 2.1) identifies the three "critical psychological states" associated with high levels of internal motivation, satisfaction, and quality of performance.[4] These psychological states are experienced meaningfulness of the work, experienced responsibility for the outcomes, and knowledge of actual results. The existence of these psychological states in a job should lead to low absenteeism and turnover and high levels of internal motivation, satisfaction, and quality of performance.

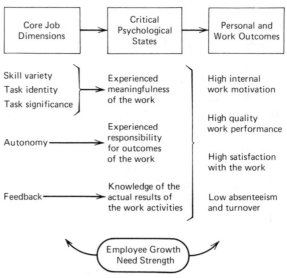

Figure 2-1   Model of Motivation

Five characteristics of the job (core job dimensions) were gathered using the survey instrument: skill variety, task identity, task significance, autonomy, and feedback. Each core dimension is defined as follows:

- **Skill Variety** The degree to which a job requires a variety of different activities and involves the use of a number of different skills and talents of the employee.

- **Task Identity** The degree to which the job requires the completion of a "whole" and identifiable piece of work—that is, doing a job from beginning to end with a visible outcome.

- **Task Significance** The degree to which the job has a substantial impact on the lives or work of other people—whether in the immediate organization or in the external environment.

- **Autonomy** The degree to which the job provides substantial freedom, independence, and discretion to the employee in scheduling his or her work and in determining the procedures to be used in carrying it out.

- **Feedback from the Job Itself** The degree to which carrying out the work activities required by the job results in the employee obtaining information about the effectiveness of his or her performance.

Table 2.1 compares employee perceptions of the five core dimensions in jobs of DP professionals in our survey versus other professions (from the Hackman/Oldham studies of over 6000 persons). The ratings for system analysts are higher than those of other professionals. So are the ratings for programmer/analysts. However, in four of the five categories, programmers rate the key job dimensions significantly lower than do other professionals.*

*Throughout this chapter, differences are significant at the p ≤ .01 level unless otherwise stated.

Table 2.1 Comparison of Core Job Dimensions Between DP and Other Professionals

Core Job Dimension	DP Professionals		Other
Factors	Analysts	Programmer/Analysts	Programmers	Professionals
Skill variety	5.55	5.45	5.23	5.36
Task identity	5.37	5.29	5.00	5.06
Task significance	5.75	5.72	5.46	5.62
Autonomy	5.31	5.48	5.13	5.35
Feedback from job	5.20	5.05	5.10	5.08

(Ratings on a scale of 7, where 1 is low and 7 is high)

The Effect of High Core Job Dimensions

Hackman and Oldham use the three "psychological states" experienced by a golfer to illustrate the effect of core dimensions. "Consider, for example, a golfer at a driving range, practicing to get rid of a hook. His activity is *meaningful* to him; he has chosen to do it because he gets a 'kick' from testing his skills by playing the game. He knows that he alone is *responsible* for what happens when he hits the ball. And he has *knowledge of the results* within a few seconds."[5]

These three psychological states are defined as follows:

1 *Experienced meaningfulness* Individuals must perceive their work as worthwhile or important by some system of values they accept.

2 *Experienced responsibility* They must believe that they personnally are accountable for the outcomes of their efforts.

3 *Knowledge of results* They must be able to determine, on some fairly regular basis, whether the outcome of their work is satisfactory.

If these conditions exist, people "tend to feel very good about themselves when they perform well." Those good feelings motivate them to try to continue to do well. This is what the behavioral scientists mean by "internal motivation"—rather than being dependent on external factors (such as incentive pay or compliments from the boss). The JDS model computes a single summary index of the "motivating potential" of a job. The index is called the motivating potential score (MPS).

When all three psychological states are high, then internal work motivation, job satisfaction, and work quality are high and absenteeism and turnover are low. Several studies by Hackman and Oldham have substantiated the conceptual model. One was a study of more than 1000 employees working on about 100 diverse jobs in more than a dozen organizations over a two-year period. The effect on absenteeism and job performance was substantial, as shown in Figure 2.2.

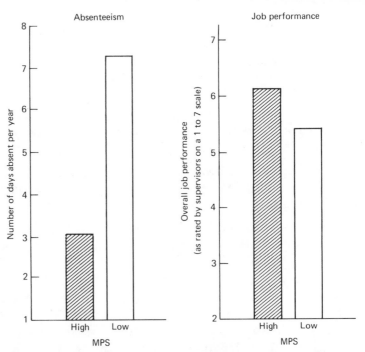

Figure 2-2 Absenteeism and job performance for employees with jobs high and low in motivating potential.[6]

Table 2.2 presents the model output on psychological states, comparing DP to other professionals. These figures are derived from Table 2.1. The results are comparable for "experienced meaningfulness." In the other two categories, DP professional scores are lower. The survey

Table 2.2 Comparison of Psychological States Resulting From Core Job Dimensions

Psychological State	DP Professionals			Other Professionals
	Analysts	Programmer/Analysts	Programmers	
Experienced meaningfulness	5.56	5.49	5.23	5.40
Experienced responsibility	5.31	5.48	5.13	5.75
Knowledge of results	4.59	4.42	4.55	5.00

(Ratings on a scale of 7, where 1 is low and 7 is high)

revealed the specific reason for the lower rating on "knowledge of results" was lack of feedback from supervision. Feedback from the job itself was approximately the same as for other professionals.

Our supervisors are not doing nearly as good a job (3.97) as their peers in other professions (4.21) in providing feedback to employees. This is an area where an immediate improvement is possible (see Chapter 6).

Measures of Satisfaction

The JDS/DP does not measure actual work outcomes: productivity, employee perceptions of their productivity, turnover, or absenteeism. Employees report directly how satisfied (or dissatisfied) they are with various aspects of their job. Table 2.3 indicates that DP professionals generally are satisfied (recall that the midpoint of the rating scale is 4.0). However, although their general satisfaction is higher than that of other professionals, they are less satisfied with supervision.

The JDS/DP proved to be an especially good discriminator. Two organizations surveyed were not "healthy" in behavioralist terms. All others were. In fact we attempted to survey organizations whose working environment was healthy, because we wanted to build "norms." In the past DP has been without benchmarks in the behavioral areas.

The unhealthy organizations were significantly below the norms on most of the core job dimensions. With the information from the VDS/DP we have a substantive basis for beginning the process of redesigning jobs in those organizations.

Table 2.3 Comparison of Satisfaction in DP and Other Professionals

Measures of Satisfaction	DP Professionals			Other Professionals
	Analysts	Programmer/Analysts	Programmers	
General satisfaction	5.10	5.37	5.30	4.88
Satisfaction with co-workers	5.01	5.22	4.96	5.48
Satisfaction with supervision	4.64	4.60	4.60	4.89

Growth Need Strength

The expectation is that people who have a high need for personal growth and development will respond more positively to a job high in motivating potential than people with low growth need strength. Obviously, not everyone is able to become internally motivated—even when the motivating potential of the job is quite high. Behavioral research has shown that the psychological needs of people determine who can (and who cannot) become internally motivated at work. Some people have strong need for personal accomplishment—for learning and developing beyond where they are now, for being stimulated and challenged, and so on. These people are high in "growth need strength" (GNS). Figure 2.3 diagrammatically shows how individual growth needs affect response to a job high in motivating potential.

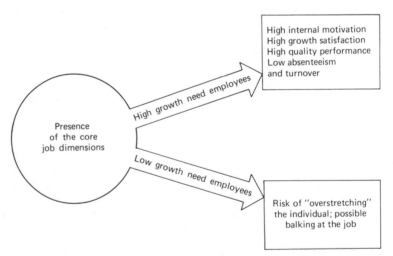

Figure 2-3 The effect of a high motivating potential job on persons with varying growth need strength.[7]

Growth need strength is high for DP professionals compared to other professionals and to other job categories. Table 2.4 shows this effect. This outcome is no surprise for DP managers used to demands by their staff that they be provided training, be allowed to attend conferences and seminars, and so on. A frequent result of behavioral research is that intuitive beliefs are substantiated. Survey data on GNS provide a good example.

However, the key reason for measuring GNS is to compare it with the job's potential to fulfill GNS. A job low in motivating potential will frustrate a person with high GNS. It is a perfect example of the old cliche of a round peg in a square hole.

The motivating potential score (MPS) shown in the right-hand column of Table 2.4 enables a comparison of the job potential to the employee GNS. MPS is a computed value (not on a scale of 7) reflecting the potential of a job for eliciting positive internal work motivation on the part of employees. The H/O survey results include an example of the imbalance of GNS and MPS. Notice in Table 2.4 that the lowest GNS is for structural work. On

Table 2.4 Comparison of GNS and MPS by Job Category

Job Category	Growth Need Strength (GNS)	Motivating Potential Score (MPS)
DP professionals	5.91	153.6
Other professionals	5.59	153.7
Sales	5.70	146.0
Service	5.38	151.7
Managerial	5.30	155.9
Clerical	4.95	105.9
Machine trades	4.82	135.8
Bench work	4.88	109.8
Processing	4.57	105.1
Structural work	4.54	140.6

the other hand, the MPS for that field is 140, which is near the midpoint for all jobs reported in the table. Jobs in that industry have a motivating potential above the growth needs of the workers. The lower arrow in Figure 2.3 illustrates this situation.

On the other hand, the upper arrow illustrates the situation for the DP professional. Both the individual's GNS and the job's MPS are high—the highest in the table. As discussed in Chapter 3, such a balance is not so prevalent among the other jobs in the DP organization.

Similarly, although the average for all organizations in our study showed a high positive correlation between GNS and MPS, this was not always the case for individual

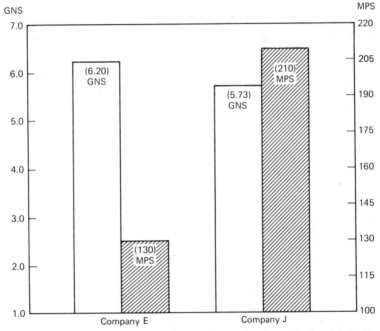

Figure 2-4   Contrast Between Two Organizations In GNS/MPS.

organizations. For example, the organization with the second highest GNS (6.20) had the lowest MPS (130), as seen in Figure 2.4 (Company E). In contrast, another organization, Company J in the figure, had the lowest GNS (5.73) and the highest MPS (210). Now that they are aware of this disparity, these organizations can analyze their jobs to reduce the inequity.

Social Need Strength

On a recent trip to Des Moines, we were forced to change planes in Lincoln, Nebraska. While we were waiting in the terminal, another passenger made a surprising seat request. He wanted to sit in the middle seat in the three-abreast arrangement of the Boeing 727. One of us asked the reservation clerk if this request was as unusual as we suspected. "First time it ever happened in my five years with the airline," he responded.

Odds are that this passenger wasn't a programmer or an analyst. The survey revealed that systems professionals have a startlingly low proclivity to social interaction.

The most surprising result of the survey was the measurement of the variable labeled "social need strength" (SNS). Survey questions related to this variable determine an individual's need to interact with others. The average score on this variable for all other professionals was 5.48. For all DP professionals in our survey, the score is 4.20 (see Figure 2.5); for five organizations the average was only 2.23. Whereas some professions attract people who have a high propensity for, and reinforcement from, interaction with others—DP does not appear to exhibit this characteristic.

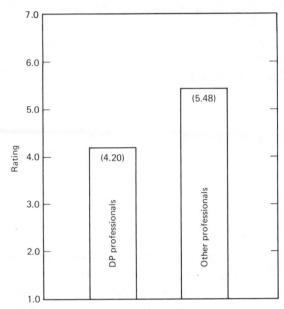

Figure 2-5   Comparison of Social Need Strength SNS

Why is the DP professional's SNS so low? We believe we have identified the principal contributor. Persons around the country with whom we have shared these ideas generally support our view.

We will begin the discussion by an analysis of students who enter our degree program in Information System Analysis and Design. Few students decide to enter that program prior to taking the introductory DP course. All students in the College of Business and Administration are required to take this course in their sophomore year. The course is almost equally divided into three subjects: (1) computing concepts, (2) computer programming, and (3) introduction to system analysis and design. The course is taught in that same sequence so students will have most of the semester to write and debug their programs.

Of the three subjects, one provides unusually good feedback on performance—computer programming. Students do not have to be told by their instructor how well they are performing this task. The task itself provides excellent feedback because of the compiler diagnostics.

About 10 percent of the students are exceptionally good programmers and the system enables them to recognize this fact—long before they have taken the midterm exam. These students also find that they do not need the assistance of others to develop their programs. Although we encourage students to work in teams, some prefer to work alone without the "hindrance" of the slower-learning team members. Not all of the better students work alone, but many do. They are bright, logical people who work well independently.

The system analysis and design portion of the course is more conceptual. Students must depend more on the final examination to provide feedback on how well they performed in this portion of the course. The best students in the course typically choose to major in information system analysis and design. However, it was the programming aspect of the course that gave them the best feedback on their suitability to this career field.

Their first course in the major is a COBOL course. It reinforces their decision on their career choice. Not until their senior year do they begin the system courses. Many are not nearly as comfortable in these courses as they were in the programming portions of the curriculum. Few change their major, however.

Company training programs are similar in structure. Those companies that train their staff from scratch begin with programming courses. Trainees who succeed in programming are permitted to remain in the company program. They can be successful in both their training course and their first job without a great deal of interaction with others. They are not antisocial. They mix well with the other programmers. But compared to personnel in other parts of the company—for example, the sales department—to be successful, programmers need far less skill in verbal communication. Nor is understanding of behavioral patterns a prerequisite to success in programming.

Reflecting on this situation, we were not surprised by the JDS/DP identification of low SNS for programmers. We *were* surprised that analysts had equally low SNS. Their job requires a great deal of interaction to ensure success.

Further reflection, however, made us realize that this situation should not have been surprising. What is the typical career path in the systems department? The path is through programming to analysis. So—employees carry their low SNS with them on up the career ladder. Chapter 4 shows that DP supervisors and managers also have much lower SNS than their counterparts in the managerial positions in the company. This situation is enigmatic since interaction with persons outside the DP department is essential to success.

The characteristic of low SNS of DP personnel may be the prime factor in the perpetual difficulty in maintaining satisfactory relations with users of DP.

We discuss this situation in more detail in subsequent chapters.

Implications of Low SNS

Analysts have increasingly been grouped into teams in anticipation that productivity will be increased. The Chief Programmer Team (C-P-T) concept has been widely publicized and advocated. Some have suggested that it is the social interaction of the team that has produced whatever productivity benefits resulted from the C-P-T approach. If our study is representative, it mandates caution in accepting such views.

What does this survey statistic mean to a manager of DP professionals? The lack of need for social interaction does not mean that teams should not be utilized. It does indicate that DP professionals are not actively seeking a team experience. Managers of other parts of the company will find their employees eager to interact—and a team approach is a natural organization to facilitate such interaction.

This conclusion is supported by data from Table 2.3. DP professionals in the survey organizations were satisfied with their co-workers. In other words, they were getting the interaction they needed—so long as it was not overdone.

The computer industry, like others, has a number of experientially derived theorems that have not previously been validated by statistical studies. For example, how often have you heard the comment that programmers are "loners"?

The GNS section of our study lent authenticity to one of those theorems. Here is another case. Perhaps the theorem is best expressed by Gerald Weinberg in his widely quoted *Psychology of Computer Programming:* "If asked, most programmers probably say they preferred to work alone in a place where they wouldn't be disturbed by other people."[8]

However, we interpret the survey results on SNS as follows: management does not need to reduce emphasis on the project team; it just needs to control the frequency and duration of team meetings. Consider the frequently cited guideline that structured walkthroughs should be limited to no more than one hour. (You don't find similar guidelines in the literature on management meetings! The SNS for managers in the H/O surveys was 5.65.) The structured walkthrough guideline was empirically derived—probably by judging the increasing level of impatience by analysts and programmers when a meeting dragged on.

Moreover, a low social need may indicate the need for additional training on supervisory techniques and joint goal-setting processes when DP professionals are promoted to management positions.

Summary of Findings

Although we have barely begun the in-depth discussion of our data base, the following tentative propositions can be identified:

DP Professionals Have Some Unique Differences from the General Population

DP professionals have substantially higher GNS than *any* of the job categories surveyed by Hackman and Oldham. This is true of analysts, programmer/analysts, and programmers. On the other hand, they have the *lowest* social need strength among professionals—and it is significantly lower.

Good Job Match is Possible

For the survey firms—intentionally selected because they are healthy—the motivating potential of the jobs match the GNS of DP professionals.

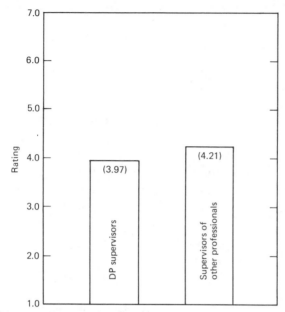

Figure 2-6   Feedback to Employees

Supervisory Feedback to Employees Can Be Improved

Employees in the firms surveyed are generally satisfied with co-workers and with supervisors. Nevertheless, they believe that feedback from supervision should be improved. They rate this category lower than do their counterparts in the other professions (see Figure 2.6).

An Appropriate Conceptual Model Exists

The Hackman/Oldham model is applicable to the computer field. Our analysis substantiated that of the original researchers, with comparable statistical reliability and validity. The conceptual model is useful for management in our

field to analyze individual motivation patterns and the
JDS/DP is useful to gather data to determine satisfaction
levels and work outcomes.

Job Redesign Has Potential

Studies of other industries by Hackman and Oldham and
by others (e.g., Rosenbach[9]) show that job redesign can
increase satisfaction and productivity. With the norms
resulting from our study, managers in the computer field
have the basis for determining which jobs have potential
for improvement.

Conclusion and Summary

Productivity improvement consists of two parts—
improving techniques and increasing motivation to utilize
those techniques. An enormous amount of time and energy
has gone into the first part—technique improvement. Why
has the second part—motivation—been given so little
attention?

Is it the qualitative nature of motivation? Are we so
oriented in the analysis of the quantitative part of the job
that we willfully ignore the harder-to-measure aspects of
employee motivation?

Or is it the fact that we are "systematic" people—who
deal in practicalities. We want something we can touch or
see. "Lines of code per hour" is a measurement that can
be substantiated. Degree of motivation cannot be seen,
felt, tasted, or smelled—but it exists.

We are emulating the industrial engineers of the 1940s
who kept chipping away at each job on the auto assembly
line until it was splintered into the ultimate level of
specialization. We seem to be concentrating just as fer-

vently on fragmenting the jobs of analysis and programming. The C-P-T concept is the latest in the long list of activities designed for enhancing specialization. The analysis/programming task now is fragmented into the elements performed by the chief programmer, the moderator, the librarian, the recorder, and so on. Perhaps jobs should be enlarged rather than reduced in scope.

If we devote equal time to the analysis of motivation and the ingredients of job satisfaction, this alone may increase productivity. However, productivity increase is the wrong reason for initiating such a study. Shouldn't a supervisor gain as much satisfaction from helping employees achieve fulfillment as from meeting cost-schedule objectives?

Fortunately, it is possible to achieve both objectives. Behavioral science researchers have proved in other industries that productivity can be increased by a better matching of jobs with individuals.

Notes

1   *Work in America,* Report of the Special Task Force to the Secretary of Health, Education and Welfare (Washington, D.C.: U.S. Government Printing Office, 1973).

2   J. R. Hackman and G. R. Oldham, "Development of the Job Diagnostic Survey," *Journal of Applied Psychology,* Vol. 60, No. 2, 1975, pp. 159–170.

*As with every instrument in use today, the JDS has its detractors. Some behavioralists question the model's predictive ability.[3] However, the behavioral scientists agree concerning the model's ability to measure motivation and job satisfaction.

3   R. M. Steers and R. T. Mowday, "The Motivational Properties of Tasks," *Academy of Management Review,* October 1977, pp. 645–658.

4   J. R. Hackman, G. R. Oldham, R. Janson, and K. Purdy, "A New Strategy for Job Enrichment," *California Management Review,* Vol. 17, No. 4, 1975, pp. 57–71.

5   Ibid., p. 58.

6 Ibid., p. 66.

7 Ibid., p. 60.

8 Gerald M. Weinberg, *The Psychology of Computer Programming* (New York: Van Nostrand Reinhold, 1971), p. 52.

9 W. E. Rosenbach, "An Evaluation of Participative Work Redesign: A Longitudinal Field Experiment," D.B.A. dissertation, University of Colorado, 1977.

3

MOTIVATING POTENTIAL FOR JOBS IN COMPUTER OPERATIONS

Hardware performance measurement is receiving a great deal of attention from today's cost-conscious management. What if management were told that its equipment was achieving only two-thirds of the performance of other organizations? There is little doubt that management would place high priority on this problem.

Would management be equally responsive if told that the motivating potential of jobs in computer operations is two-thirds of that of the jobs in the systems department?

This is not a hypothetical situation. Our national survey shows that employees in DP operations perceive their jobs to be deficient in the key characteristics that produce motivation and lead to increased productivity. The motivating potential score (MPS) of these jobs is lower than that of *any* of the other 500 jobs in the Hackman/ Oldham data base.

The research leads us to conclude that computer operations has a "stepchild" status in the DP organization. It seems to require the "sledgehammer" effect of a catastrophic event such as a flood or bombing to draw attention to computer operations. Remember the perhaps apocryphal but oft-repeated story of the ICBM that had to be destroyed because it veered off course as a result of a keypunch error in its guidance system?

Yet few would argue with the statement that the success of a computer application is just as dependent on the people in data entry, data control, and computer operations as it is on the designers and programmers. However, it's design and programming activities that typically receive the spotlight.

Comparisons with Systems Personnel

Table 3.1 lists perceptions of computer operations personnel in the national survey described in Chapter 2. Over 1200 operations people participated in the survey. In four of the five core job dimensions, ratings are significantly lower* than those of programmers and analysts. Only in the area of task significance are the ratings similar for the

Table 3.1 Ratings of Personnel in Computer Operations Compared to Programmers and Analysts on Core Job Dimensions

	Computer Operations Employees	Programmers and Analysts
Skill variety	3.98	5.41
Task identity	4.53	5.21
Task significance	5.62	5.61
Autonomy	4.08	5.29
Feedback from job	4.62	5.13

(Scale: 1 through 7, with 7 representing the most desirable rating.)

*Throughout this chapter differences are significant at the $p \le .01$ level.

two groups of employees. In this category, operations supervisors are doing a good job in conveying to their employees the importance of their work.

However, the ratings are critically deficient in the other core job dimensions. Not only are the ratings low when compared to the systems department, they are also low when compared to other jobs in the company.

Comparisons to Other Occupations

Table 3.2 compares the ratings of operations personnel to white- and blue-collar workers in the Hackman/Oldham data base. The ratings of operations personnel on the five core job dimensions are: skill variety (3.98), task identity (4.53), task significance (5.62), autonomy (4.08), and feedback from the job (4.62).

The H/O figures are separated into white-collar and blue-collar workers and represent the following industries: structural work, bench work, machine trades, processing, service, sales, and clerical.

The summary of the H/O data for white-collar workers shows higher ratings than computer operations personnel

Table 3.2 Ratings of Personnel in Computer Operators Compared to White- and Blue-Collar Workers on Core Job Dimensions

Core Job Dimension Factors	Computer Operations Employees	Other Occupations	
		White Collar	Blue Collar
Skill variety	3.98	4.74	4.49
Task identity	4.53	4.76	4.60
Task significance	5.62	5.47	5.55
Autonomy	4.08	4.85	4.83
Feedback from job	4.62	4.88	4.76

in four of the five core job dimensions. Only in task significance are the ratings higher for operations personnel.

Table 3.3 presents the mean ratings on psychological states. These ratings are derived from responses on the core job dimensions plus questions concerning feedback from peers and from supervisors. All the ratings of DP operations personnel are significantly below those for white- and blue-collar workers. Ratings are well below 5 on the scale of 7. Only one rating of the white-collar workers (knowledge of results, 4.93) is below 5. All ratings of blue-collar workers are above 5.

Figure 3.1 shows the MPS of operations jobs compared to some of the other jobs in the H/O data base. Recall from Chapter 2 that MPS is a three-digit figure computed from other scores in the survey. The MPS for operations jobs is lower than *any* job in the H/O data base.

These tables reveal the huge potential for improving jobs in the operations area. Productivity can be increased significantly be restructing jobs in that area. Before explaining how that might be accomplished, let us examine other data from the survey of operations personnel.

Table 3.3 Computer Operations Compared to Other Occupations on Critical Psychological Factors

Psychological State	Computer Operations Employees	Other Occupations	
		White Collar	Blue Collar
Experienced meaningfulness	4.71	5.10	5.14
Experienced responsibility	4.08	5.46	5.38
Knowledge of results	4.33	4.93	5.09

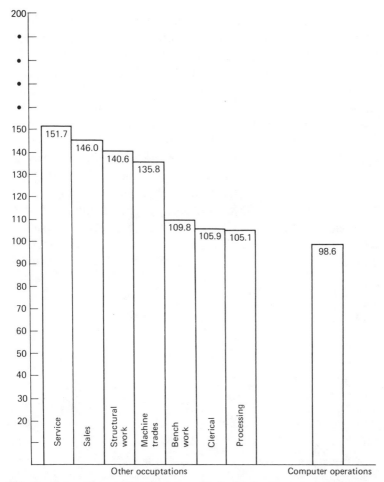

Figure 3-1 The motivating potential of jobs in computer operations, as they are presently designed, is below that of other occupations. Motivating potential score (MPS) is computed from the employee ratings on job factors.

Growth Need Strength

The GNS of operations personnel is very high compared to both blue- and white-collar workers. Figure 3.2 shows that the GNS of operations personnel is 5.78 compared to 5.19 for white-collar workers and 4.74 for blue-collar workers.

It is not clear why operations personnel have such high growth need. It applies for all three categories, however: operators (5.80), data control (5.90), and data entry (5.61). Apparently the dynamic characteristics of the DP industry appeal to people who are willing and interested in growth opportunities. Unfortunately, operations people do not feel challenged by the work in their department. Figure 3.2 clearly shows the low MPS of jobs in operations compared to those of white- and blue-collar workers. MPS for operations is lower than that of any of the 500 jobs in the H/O data base. It is the only one below the 100 level. White-

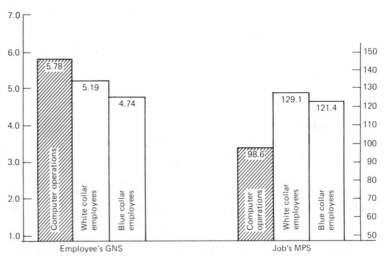

Figure 3-2 Comparison of MPS/GNS for Operations Personnel vs Other Occupations

collar MPS (129.1) and blue-collar MPS (121) are significantly higher.

Figure 3.3 shows that GNS for operations personnel is much closer to that of programmers and analysts than it is to other workers. However, from a statistical standpoint, the difference between programmers and analysts (5.91) and operations personnel (5.78) is significant. The startling difference, reflected by the right side of Figure 3.3, is in MPS. The MPS for operations personnel is two-thirds that of systems department personnel.

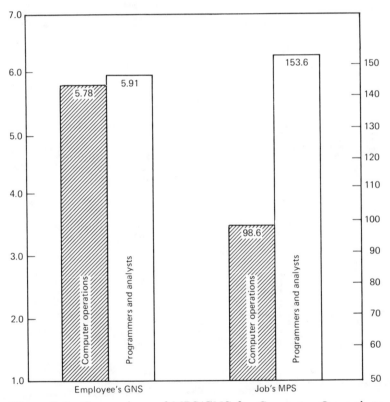

Figure 3-3 Comparison of MPS/GNS for Computer Operations vs. the Systems Department

The gap between growth need and growth satisfaction is clearly revealed on the left side of Figure 3.4: operators, 5.80 GNS versus 4.63 GS; data control, 5.90 GNS versus 4.84 GS; and data entry, 5.61 versus 4.18 GS.

Social Need Strength

The right side of Figure 3.4 compares social satisfaction to social need. SNS for data control personnel is 5.51 compared to social satisfaction of 5.48. For the other two jobs

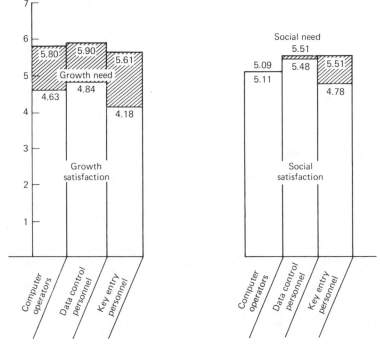

Figure 3-4 Growth Need vs Growth Satisfaction and Social Need vs Social Satisfaction for Computer Operations Personnel

the satisfaction level is well below the need level: operators, 5.09 SNS versus 5.11 social satisfaction; and data entry, 5.51 SNS versus 4.78 social satisfaction.

A surprising difference is that between operations personnel and systems personnel, SNS for the two groups is as follows:

$$\text{operations personnel} = 5.53$$

$$\text{programmers and analysts} = 4.20$$

Measures of Satisfaction

The figures in Table 3.4 might appear to contradict data in earlier tables and figures. Operations personnel in the survey firms are above the midpoint in four of the five categories of satisfaction measurement. Only in pay satis-

Table 3.4 Satisfaction Levels of Operations Personnel versus Other Occupations

Measures of Satisfaction	Computer Operations Personnel			Other Occupations	
	Computer Operators	Key Entry Personnel	Data Control Personnel	White Collar	Blue Collar
General satisfaction	5.01	4.76	5.18	4.60	4.80
Pay satisfaction	4.19	4.20	4.38	4.19	4.40
Security satisfaction	5.00	4.65	5.34	4.83	4.76
Social satisfaction	5.11	4.78	5.48	5.33	5.40
Supervisory satisfaction	5.10	5.02	5.24	4.95	4.79

faction is the rating below a level of 5 for all three groups. Compared to workers studied by Hackman and Oldham, DP operations personnel in the survey firms are more satisfied.

Measuring satisfaction levels alone, the approach in some surveys, might lead one to expect high productivity in DP operations. However, as measures of job characteristics show, general satisfaction levels can be relatively independent of the job's motivating potential. Behavioral scientists have shown that general satisfaction and productivity are not necessarily related.[1] There are cases of organizations with low productivity despite high general satisfaction levels.

Why are DP employee perceptions of general satisfaction so high when their ratings on core job dimensions are so low? Three possible reasons are:

1   A good career path exists in DP operations (plenty of latitude within each job category plus longitudinal growth possibilities to other functions within the DP operations department).

2   Promotional opportunities occur frequently because of the accelerated growth of the DP department compared to other departments in the company.

3   Pay satisfaction is high enough to partially offset the lack of challenge in the job.

In other words, employees are not unhappy "biding their time" in present jobs—in anticipation of promotion to better jobs in a fast-moving career field.

Imagine the productivity potential if jobs could be redesigned to increase MPS to a level comparable to GNS of the job incumbents?

Need to Improve Feedback

Figure 3.5 indicates that operations personnel in all three categories believe that feedback needs improvement. Two ratings are below the midpoint of the scale: computer operators (3.95) and data control (3.92). Data entry is only a little higher (4.09).

Blue- and white-collar workers in the H/O surveys also believe feedback can be improved. White-collar ratings

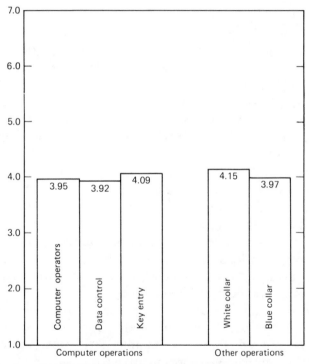

Figure 3-5   Feedback from Supervisors

were higher (4.15) than blue-collar ratings (3.97), but both are low compared to ratings on the satisfaction categories.

The relatively high ratings on supervisory satisfaction (Table 3.4) indicate that feedback problems are not serious enough to jeopardize supervisor/employee relations. However, the employees make it clear by their ratings that they believe feedback can be improved. Recommendations for approaches to improving feedback are provided in Appendix III.

Conclusions

How does one evaluate the low ratings on core job dimensions by employees in our survey organizations? Why are they significantly below the ratings of employees in other occupations studied by Hackman and Oldham? Or, discounting other occupations, why are so many of the ratings of DP operations personnel below the midpoint of the rating scale?

One answer could be that our survey firms were not representative of the DP field. In our national survey, we purposely sought to study normal organizations. We wanted firms to be representative of the broad spectrum of the DP field—neither subordinate nor inferior compared to other organizations. In this way we hoped to establish norms against which managers of other organizations could evaluate their jobs and employees.

We used an instrument whose reliability and validity had already been substantiated. Our own statistical analysis proved that our sample size was sufficient. But—was our sample representative?

We sought to ensure representativeness by discussing our potential survey organizations with people outside those organizations, such as officers in local DP professional societies and managers of other DP departments in the city. This process is imperfect—we were forced to eliminate some organizations after interviews with their managers and employees. Careful comparison of the data, organization by organization, and of the standard deviations on the means of the combined survey convinces us that our survey is statistically sound.

If so, the resulting question is, "What can we do to improve jobs in the DP operations area?" Can we, at least, raise all ratings on the core job dimensions above the midpoint of the scale—the "moderately acceptable" level as perceived by employees? A not-unrealistic target is to raise ratings to the level of workers in other occupations.

Operations personnel are quite different from employees in the systems department, as revealed by SNS and GNS ratings. Supervisors in these areas need to use different management and motivation techniques.

More important than the difference in GNS and SNS is the difference in MPS as perceived by the two groups of employees. Operations personnel, with high GNS compared to white- and blue-collar workers, believe their jobs to be lacking the key factors for motivation.

Management needs to consider the potential benefits of work redesign—proven in other fields.

Potential Improvements Through Work Redesign

Richard Hackman wrote in the *Harvard Business Review:*

> Work redesign can help individuals regain that kick that comes from doing a job well and encourage them to care enough about their work to develop the competence to do it even better. These payoffs from work redesign will go

well beyond simple job satisfaction. Cows grazing in a field may be satisfied, and organizations can keep employees just as satisfied by paying them well, keeping bosses off their backs, and arranging things so the days pass without undue stress or strain.

This is not the kind of satisfaction at issue here. It is a satisfaction that develops only when an individual is stretching and growing as a human being and increasing his sense of competence and worth.[2]

Two terms used frequently by managers and authors when discussing work redesign are job enrichment and job enlargement. *Job enrichment* refers to a planned change of job content to provide the worker with a greater variety of work that requires a higher level of knowledge or skill generally providing an opportunity for personal growth and development. In a job enrichment program, a worker is encouraged to participate in the planning, organizing, and controlling of work as contrasted with the doing of work.

In a *job enlargement* program the worker is given a greater variety of work (such as job rotation) without increasing the need for a higher level of knowledge and skills. Job enlargement does not emphasize the autonomy or responsibility dimension of the work; it concentrates on the horizontal aspects of the job. For purposes of discussion in this article, both terms are included within the definition of work redesign.

In our notes section we cite research that substantiates the value of work redesign and shows the importance of employee participation in the process. However, some well-known behavioralists, such as Frederick Herzberg, argue that employees are not qualified to participate in making changes in their work. We disagree. We believe that there is no better expert on work redesign than the person doing the work. On the other hand, employees will not be motivated to participate in work redesign without supportive management.

A classic experiment with participation was undertaken at the Marion, Virginia, plant of the Harwood Manufacturing company.[3] In the company's pajama factory, change was introduced in manufacturing procedures and the degree of involvement in the change effort by the workers was controlled. Two "full-participation" groups were given an explanation of the change and then participated with management in implementing the change. A third group participated in the change effort on a limited basis, and a fourth group was only given an explanation of the change effort.

The carefully designed experiment showed that post-change productivity improvements were directly related to the degree of participation. Further, as participation in the decision-making process increased, disruption and turnover from the change effort decreased.

In 1967 Texas Instruments[4] started a work redesign program for 600 female assemblers of navigation equipment. The assemblers worked in small groups and each group was asked by management to help set production goals. The assemblers were given cost information, terms of the government contracts such as quality requirements, production schedules, and delivery schedules. At the end of one year assembly time decreased from 138 to 32 hours. The company also reported a reduction in absenteeism, turnover, complaints, and trips to the medical center.

Texas Instruments also implemented job enrichment as a result of poor performance of contract janitors and decided to bring the function under company control and direction. The job enrichment effort consisted of supplying better cleaning equipment, selecting and training of personnel with more care, increasing communication and feedback, and improving wages and fringe benefits. The results were a 20 percent increase in cleanliness ratings, a 40 percent decrease in the number of janitors required to do the work, and a 91 percent decrease in quarterly turnover.

During the early 1970s Travelers Insurance Company[5] decided to attempt to enrich the jobs of keypunch operators because the department was plagued by high error rates, high absenteeism, high turnover, and low morale. This is one of the few reported work redesign efforts in a DP function.* The jobs were diagnosed by using the JDS. This diagnosis indicated that the keypunch workers perceived their jobs to be extremely low on all five core job dimensions. The job was changed to permit the workers to be responsible for their own accounts and to directly interface with their clients. Incorrect work was returned directly to the operator who had accomplished it. Reports on productivity and error rates were provided on a weekly basis directly to concerned workers.

The job enrichment effort produced some amazing results: a 39.6 percent increase in productivity for the experimental group, whereas the control group increased only 8.1 percent. The number of workers was reduced from 98 to 60 through attrition. The error rate decreased from 1.53 percent to 0.99 percent. Job satisfaction in the experimental group improved 16.5 percent; in the control group it improved ½ of one percent. Absenteeism in the experimental group *decreased* 24.1 percent while it *increased* 29 percent in the control group. The bottom line payoff was a hard saving of $64,305 during the experiment.

---

*Rolls Royce is also attempting to enrich the jobs of data entry operators.

Recommendations

For a decision to be effective, it not only must be a correct decision, it must be implemented properly. The persons assigned to implement it must be committed. These relationships can be expressed in the formula

$$ED = RD \times CD$$

Effective decision (ED) is the result of the right decision (RD) times commitment to the decision (CD) by the implementers. Some managers concentrate almost exclusively on the middle term of the formula and underestimate the importance of the third term. Commitment can be enhanced when subordinates and/or team members participate—are actively involved—in the decision-making process. Further, in soliciting participation, the manager must be sincere. The manager must believe that a good solution requires involvement of the people who implement the decision. Workers cannot be manipulated for very long. They soon "see through" a manipulative manager.

However, participation alone does not ensure success. The method by which suggestions are solicited and processed and feedback is given are the keys to success or failure in participative work redesign. The procedure for work redesign is provided in Appendix IV. Feedback will be discussed in more detail in Chapter 6.

Notes

1 C. H. Greene, "The Satisfaction-Performance Controversy," *Business Horizons*, Vol. 15, No. 2, pp. 31–41.

2 J. Richard Hackman, "Is Job Enrichment Just a Fad?" *Harvard Business Review,* 1975, 53, p. 138.

3 L. Coch, and J. P. R. French, Jr., "Overcoming Resistance to Change," *Human Relations,* Vol. 1, 1948, pp. 512–532.

4 E. D. Weed, "Job Enrichment 'Cleans up' at Texas Instruments," in J. R. Mather, ed., *New Perspectives in Job Enrichment* (New York: Van Nostrand Reinhold, 1971).

5 J. R. Hackman, G. R. Oldham, R. Janson, and K. Purdy, "A New Strategy for Job Enrichment," *California Management Review,* Vol. 17, No. 4, 1975, pp. 57–71. Also see William E. Rosenbach, Robert A. Zawacki, and Cyril P. Morgan, "Research Round-up," *The Personnel Administrator,* October 1977, pp. 51–61.

MOTIVATION LEVELS OF DATA PROCESSING MANAGERS COMPARED TO THOSE OF THEIR EMPLOYEES

Background of the Survey

We obtained permission from the SMIS, (Society for Management Information Systems) Executive Council for a survey of membership. As a result, our data base contains data on more than 800 DP managers. The number of responses at the lowest level—project managers—was too small for statistical significance, so those data have been excluded. The three levels included in this report are (1) vice presidents and directors, (2) department managers, and (3) section chiefs and supervisors.

The S.M.I.S. survey was validated against two other sources of data: (1) a sample of managers who are members of DPMA (Data Processing Management Association), and (2) management in more than 50 organizations where the job diagnostic survey was administered to all computer personnel. We wanted to be able to compare perceptions of people in our profession to those in other professions and we hypothesized that there were significant differences. This hypothesis was substantiated in a national survey of analysts, programmers, and computer operations personnel. The results are reported in Chapters 2 and 3.

After establishing national norms for nonsupervisory personnel (Appendices VI, VII), we undertook the study of DP management. Our hypothesis was similar to the previous one—that the perceptions of DP managers (at all levels) are significantly different from those in other management areas.

To preserve the integrity of the JDS, the general questions on the original instrument were left unchanged. Questions relating specifically to the computer field were added to the JDS in 1977, prior to our first national survey. We also incorporated JDS questions established and validated in earlier studies by W. E. Rosenbach[1], who expanded the JDS to cover goalsetting and organizational climate.

Our research results extend the theories of motivation that originated with the work of Frederick Herzberg in the late 1950s.[2] This branch of behavioral science has concentrated on demonstrating that the primary determinants of employee satisfaction and motivation are factors intrinsic to the work itself (recognition, achievement, responsibility, advancement, personal growth in competence; this theory is discussed in Chapter 5).

In the ensuing 15 years, the theory evolved into practical application through the contributions of a number of researchers and research projects, principally those of R. N. Ford,[3] A. N. Turner and P. R. Lawrence,[4] and L. E. Davis.[5]

Building on this reservoir of research, Hackman and Oldham developed a model of job characteristics.[6] We have modified the graphic model so the survey data can be related directly to the model components (see Figure 4.1).

Manager Ratings: Job Dimensions

The data presented in Figure 4.1 are the ratings of DP managers compared to those of general management. The general data come from the Hackman/Oldham data base.

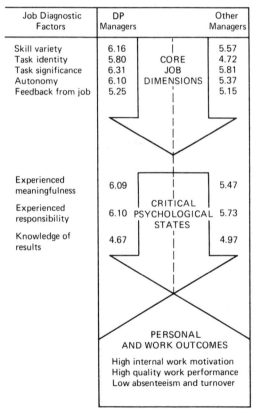

Job Diagnostic Factors	DP Managers		Other Managers
Skill variety	6.16		5.57
Task identity	5.80	CORE	4.72
Task significance	6.31	JOB	5.81
Autonomy	6.10	DIMENSIONS	5.37
Feedback from job	5.25		5.15
Experienced meaningfulness	6.09		5.47
Experienced responsibility	6.10	CRITICAL PSYCHOLOGICAL STATES	5.73
Knowledge of results	4.67		4.97

PERSONAL
AND WORK OUTCOMES

High internal work motivation
High quality work performance
Low absenteeism and turnover

Figure 4-1   Conceptual Model of Motivation

As in the case of the other surveys, all ratings are on a scale of 7 (where 7 is high and 1 is low).

There is a statistically significant difference* in DP management versus general management ratings in four of the five job dimensions. DP managers perceive their jobs to be richer in the core job dimensions in every category except feedback from the job.

DP manager ratings on the psychological states are also high in two of the three categories. The average rating is over 6 for experienced meaningfulness and experienced responsibility. The significantly lower average rating on knowledge of results (4.67) is based on two kinds of feedback: (1) from the job (core dimension 5) and (2) from managers. Feedback from the job is rated high (5.25) but feedback from managers is rated low, near the midpoint of the scale. This problem will be analyzed later in this chapter.

In Figure 4.1 data are consolidated for all management levels. Although these are average ratings, the standard deviations are low. The largest standard deviation (.94) was for the category of feedback from the job. Standard deviations for all eight categories in Figure 4.1 also varied little by the levels of management.

Comparison of Managers and Subordinates

Space limitations prohibit repeating results from the survey of analysts, programmers, and operations personnel. Ratings of DP managers for all eight categories were significantly higher than those of subordinates.

---

*Throughout this chapter, the differences are all significant at the $p \leq .01$ level, unless otherwise stated.

Satisfaction Levels

Figure 4.2 presents survey data on satisfaction levels. The differences between DP and other managers are significant except for pay satisfaction.

DP managers rate general satisfaction higher (5.5) than other managers (4.9). They rate supervisory satisfaction lower (4.1) than other managers (5.2). There is not a significant difference within management levels, however.

Standard deviation is much higher in the satisfaction categories than any other measurement category (e.g., 1.43 for supervisory satisfaction). The same general pattern is true for non-DP managers.

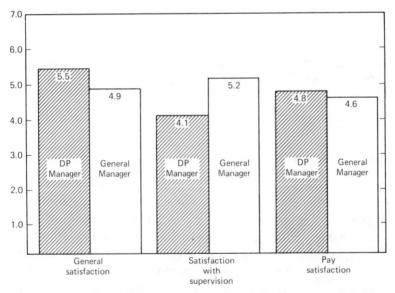

Figure 4-2 The difference in pay satisfaction is not significant. The others are significant. DP managers are less satisfied with supervision but have better general satisfaction.

High Growth Need

A valuable feature of the JDS/DP is its ability to identify a person's "growth need strength." GNS is a measure of individuals' need for personal accomplishment, for learning and developing beyond where they are now, and for being stimulated and challenged.

One of the significant findings of the national study of analysts and programmers was that the mean GNS was higher than that of any of the 500 jobs studied by Hackman and Oldham.

The same is true of their bosses. On the scale of 7, DP managers rate their need for growth at 6.32 (left side of Figure 4.3). For other managers the mean rating is 5.30. The standard deviations are low (less than .8 for both DP and other managers). GNS varies little between levels of DP management.

The high GNS of DP managers has some important implications. To properly assess these implications, data on other survey variables must be reviewed.

Highly Motivating Jobs (MPS)

MPS for managerial jobs in the DP field is significantly higher than that of any of the 500 jobs studied by Hackman and Oldham.

The right side of Figure 4.3 shows MPS for DP managers at a very high level (199.1) compared to other managers (155.9).

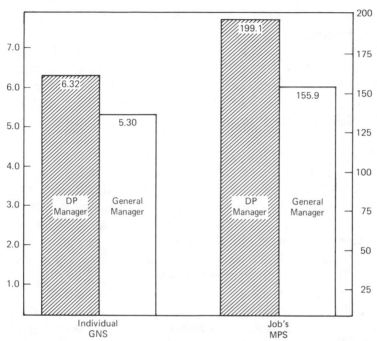

Figure 4-3 A good match exists between individual growth need of DP managers and their job's motivating potential. A similar situation exists for other managers, though both variables reflect lower values.

Matching MPS and GNS

The objective of job satisfaction and productivity improvement is to match GNS and MPS. Persons with high growth need should be working in jobs with high motivating potential. When a good match occurs, a "healthy" work environment exists and the positive outcomes identified in Figure 4.1 should result: high internal work motivation, high-quality work performance, low absenteeism and turnover.

Figure 4.3 reveals a good match between GNS and MPS—for both DP managers and other managers. A question naturally arises in analyzing Figure 4.3: Is the DP manager's job too rich? Are DP managers overstretched? GNS is 19 percent higher and MPS 28 percent higher for DP managers.

For example, the JDS/DP revealed a mismatch in several companies in one of the industries where the research took place. The promotional path traditionally has been from operations to programming. Growth needs of persons in operations are lower than those of persons in the system development area. In this company, programmer jobs were too rich. Personnel were overstretched. They were frustrated and productivity was low.

One remedial measure is reducing the scope of the job. Another is to change the promotional policy to be more selective. Instead of rigid adherence to this policy, promotions into programming could be made selectively for those persons whose growth needs are similar to the national norm for programmers.

Figure 4.4 shows a mismatch in the opposite direction. The figure contrasts the motivational environment of two of the companies in which the JDS/DP was administered. The data resulted from responses of first-line supervision in the two companies. The companies are in the same industry and are similar in terms of size and experience with computers. An "unhealthy" work environment exists for Company X; there is a serious mismatch between these supervisors' need for growth and the job's ability to motivate them. Note that the motivating potential for the job for Company X is only 60 percent of that of Company Y. The growth need strength for both groups is essentially the same.

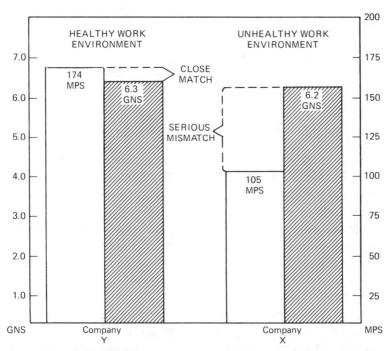

Figure 4-4 Comparison of GNS and MPS for operations super-visors in 2 companies. Work redesign is needed in company X.

Job analysis and work redesign can produce a better match of GNS and MPS. The work redesign procedures utilized by the authors are detailed in Appendix IV.

Returning to the question of a possible mismatch for DP managers, use of GNS and MPS data by themselves shows a cause for concern. MPS was 28 percent higher than that of other managers, whereas GNS was only 19 percent higher. However, positive data on the other survey variables show that such a conclusion is unwarranted.

Low Social Need (SNS)

A particularly important survey finding concerns DP managers' need for social interaction. It is much lower than
that of other managers. The mean rating in this category is
only 4.51, two-thirds that of other managers.

The term "social need strength" (SNS) refers to the
need to interact with others on the job. In this characteristic, the DP managers are more like subordinates than
peers. SNS for analysts and programmers is even lower
(4.20).

Since supervisors are promoted from the programmer
and analyst ranks, continuance of the low SNS should not
be surprising. Surprising or not, the results have important
implications in three areas: (1) the effectiveness of communication with others on the company management
team; (2) the effectiveness of communication within the
computer department—with both superiors and subordinates; and (3) the ability to have effective joint goalsetting
sessions with subordinates.

It should be noted that standard deviation is high in this
category, averaging a .99. However, SNS varies little
between managerial levels. Standard deviations are essentially the same for each of the three DP management
levels.

Some possible ramifications of low SNS will be discussed in the conclusions to this chapter.

Need for Improved Feedback

Supervisory feedback needs considerable improvement, as
seen in Figure 4.5. It is near the midpoint of the scale,
contrasting significantly with the other survey ratings.

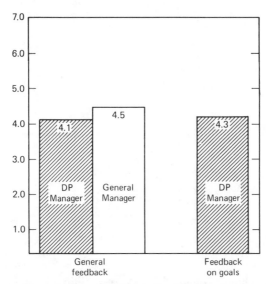

Figure 4-5 Supervisory feedback needs improvement, in general and specifically on goal performance. The Hackman/Oldham survey did not include questions concerning goals. Data is available only for DP managers.

Only one column is shown on feedback on goals because the Hackman/Oldham JDS did not include questions concerning goalsetting participation and feedback.

The degree of the problem is inversely proportional to the level in the organization. As organizational level diminishes, the magnitude of the problem increases. Figure 4.6 reflects this condition. First-line supervisors perceive their feedback as highly unsatisfactory. Tools and techniques for improving feedback and communication are discussed in Chapter 6 and Appendix III.

Feedback on goal accomplishment is somewhat better, but is low relative to ratings on other variables. Again, ratings vary by management level. Standard deviations are high, as shown in each block.

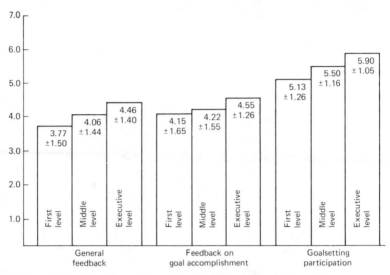

Figure 4-6 Quality of feedback varies indirectly with management level. The same condition applies to participation in goal setting.

Analysts and programmers rate feedback on goals even lower (analysts, 4.08; programmer/analysts, 3.87; programmers, 3.86).

These data indicate the absence of a role model on feedback, from the top of the management hierarchy on down.

At first glance, the higher average ratings on goalsetting participation may appear inconsistent with those on feedback on goal performance. On the other hand, the difference is not inconsistent with patterns in many firms concerning implementation of joint goalsetting programs. Considerable attention is focused on goalsetting at the start of each new fiscal year. Attention and interest fall off as the end of the year approaches. It is more exciting to discuss potentials than to face reasons for lack of goal attainment—particularly when they must be related to an individual's performance.

Implications on Interactions with Peers

Survey results indicate that DP managers possess characteristics more similar to those of their subordinates than of their peers. Their high growth need and low social need may inhibit communication—both with subordinates and with peers in other parts of the company.

Low need for social interaction may be one cause for the feedback problems evidenced by the survey. It may also cause DP managers to be frustrated over lengthy and unorganized staff meetings that they are continually required to attend. Their peers may gain reinforcement from meetings because their higher social needs are met through such activities. Also, their peers may be more effective at these meetings because of their better understanding of the emotional (social) dimension of a group.

High need for growth may intensify this problem. DP managers perceive a need to be continually stimulated and challenged. Their high-technology field provides such a stimulus. They must spend a great deal of time in study, updating their technical skills. They must spend time with vendors—in training and in evaluating hardware and software. They have less time for interaction with peers. As a result of these two differences, the DP managers may be viewed by his peers as more of "a technician" than a member of the management team. These characteristics may be the primary reason that few MIS executives are promoted into senior management positions.

Implications on Interactions with Subordinates

The feedback problem, perceived at all points of the organizational hierarchy, may also be caused by the unique characteristics of personnel in the computer field.

Persons with low social need could be expected to interact less with subordinates. And communication skill may not come naturally for such persons. Contrast such a person with one with high social need—someone in the sales organization. Persons to whom communication is easy and natural gravitate to such fields—where a great deal of interaction is required.

The following suggestions may lessen the negative effects:

1 Persons who do not inherently possess communication skills can acquire them. Formal training in both behavioral concepts and communication techniques can aid in offsetting the negative effects of low social need.

2 Departments where feedback is not produced naturally—because of low SNS of personnel—need more formalized feedback procedures. Training in effective feedback approaches can improve application of the procedure.

3 Persons with high growth need must be provided substantive training programs and challenging jobs.

Survey instruments such as the JDS/DP can aid an organization in diagnosing and analyzing its personnel and its jobs.

Conclusions

Behavioral studies rarely uncover any new truths—they merely substantiate heuristic assumptions.

Similarly, the low social need and high growth need of DP personnel may not be surprising to observers of the DP profession. What *is* surprising is the degree to which DP personnel differ from their peers in other parts of the company.

Now that some hard data on the degree of difference are known, DP managers can consider action to ensure that these differences do not have negative effects.

A very healthy motivational environment exists for DP management. Attention can be focused on the two problem areas, low social need strength and lack of feedback, with a reasonable expectation of rapid resolutions.

Notes

1 W. E. Rosenbach, "An Evaluation of Participative Work Redesign: A Longitudinal Field Experiment," D.B.A. dissertation, University of Colorado, 1977.

2 Frederick Herzberg, F. Mausner, and B. Snyderman, *The Motivation to work* (New York: Wiley, 1959).

3 R. N. Ford, *Motivation Through the Work Itself* (New York: American Management Association, 1969).

4 A. N. Turner and P. R. Lawrence, *Industrial Jobs and the Worker,* Harvard Graduate School of Business Administration, 1965.

5 L. E. Davis, "Job Design: Overview and Future Directions," *Journal of Contemporary Business,* Vol. 6, No. 2, 1978, pp. 85–102.

6 J. R. Hackman, G. R. Oldham, R. Janson, and K. Purdy, "A New Strategy for Job Enrichment," *California Management Review,* Vol. 17, No. 4, 1975, pp. 57–71.

5

MOTIVATING PEOPLE AT WORK

Earlier in this book we reported that DP professionals have the higher GNS than any of the 500 jobs surveyed by Hackman and Oldham. People in this field are obviously highly motivated. What job dimensions or factors account for this high level of motivation?

Before we discuss motivating DP people in an organization, we believe it is necessary to have a general understanding of the term "motivation." Supervisors, parents, teachers, and counselors are constantly charged with the responsibility of motivating others. Ideally, that sounds like a worthwhile goal; in practice it is difficult to accomplish because of the elusive nature of the word "motivation." The word motivation is similar to the words desire, want, need, and drive.

Motivation cannot be seen, felt, heard or smelled yet its existence is undisputed. Academics have labeled those things "concepts." A diagram of the concept of motivation may be a helpful starting point toward a definition (Figure 5.1).

Linked to the definition of motivation are three basic assumptions:[1]

1 Human behavior is caused.
2 Human behavior is goal oriented.
3 Human behavior is motivated.

Needs and Tension Begin the Motivation Process

People begin the behavior process with a felt need that produces tension within their body. This tension may be the need for food, sex, power, achievement, or just a car. Using the example of a car, people may realize the need because (1) they ride the bus to work while everyone else drives a personal automobile, (2) their present car is in need of repairs and has high mileage, or (3) a new automobile is perceived by them as a means of favorably impressing their friends.

We Search the Environment

Once aware of the need (tension), people begin a search process of the ways of satisfying the need. In the car example, the person with the need can visit a number of new car showrooms and make some comparisons. They may compare Fords, Buicks, Chryslers, and Volvos. During the search phase, persons may subjectively rank order the cars based on their perceptions of each car and how each car will meet their perceived needs. An important point is that a motivator must be *perceived* as a motivator

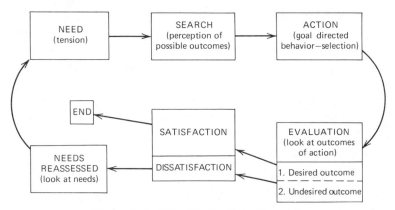

Figure 5-1 The Motivation Concept

by the person with the need before it is truly a motivator of behavior. All too often, managers believe they know what motivates their subordinates when indeed a manager's perception is different from a subordinate's perception. The following story emphasizes our point:

Wrong Reward

Dr. Charles H. Hollenberg, physician-in-chief of Toronto General Hospital, spoke recently to a group of doctors about the use of behavior modification theory in treating obesity. According to the Medical Tribune, Dr. Hollenberg related the incident of a female psychologist who attempted to encourage her overweight husband to slim down by using a reward system. The reward that she decided to use to reinforce his slimming program was her "romantic availability" in the evening.

"One can only hope," Dr. Hollenberg said, "that the therapist retained her scientific objectivity when her husband gained 10 pounds in the next three weeks."[2]

People Take Action

After searching for solutions for our need, we rank order the cars according to our subjectively calculated probability of each car satisfying our need. Then we purchase the car with the highest probability of meeting that need. This is goal-directed behavior. Goal-directed behavior is determined by the need with the greatest strength at the time a person is making a decision (see Figure 5.2). For example, the need may be for a car that performs at above 20 miles per gallon of gas, is comfortable to drive, and is perceived by family and friends as an above-average status car. Subjectively the buyer ranks this above a vacation, television set, etc.

Evaluation of the Choice

After selecting a certain car, for example, a Volvo, the owner constantly evaluates that car to see if it meets his or her expectations. In the evaluation process the owner looks at the performance (mileage, repair costs, luxury,

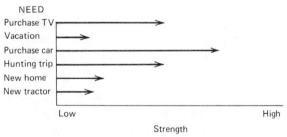

Figure 5-2   Motive Strength

etc.) of the car and subjectively compares it to the performance of other makes of car. Now a unique process may take place in the owner's mind if he or she begins to believe that the Volvo does not meet expectations. This process is known as *cognitive dissonance*. In this example the purchaser begins to receive inputs that are in conflict with expectations. These new inputs are in conflict with the previous inputs and tension is created in the mind of the purchaser. This tension is psychologically uncomfortable. Leon Festinger[3] has come forth with a theory of how the purchaser may reduce this tension. Because the state of cognitive dissonance is uncomfortable, the purchaser will attempt to reduce dissonance and to achieve more balance in his or her mind (cognitive system). Methods of reducing this cognitive dissonance are:

1 The purchaser can ignore the new inputs that do not agree with original expectations (inputs).

2 The purchaser can recognize the new inputs but rationalize the accuracy of the new inputs. "I am only getting 17 miles per gallon of gas but almost all of my driving is in the city."

3 The purchaser can accept the blame. "I did not check into mileage before I made the decision."

4 The purchaser can blame someone else. "The salesperson did not give me accurate information on gas mileage."

5 The purchaser can accept the inputs as accurate and regret the purchase. "I really didn't want a Volvo anyway—next time I will purchase an American built car."

All of these techniques are methods of coping with uncomfortable feelings that the purchaser has about himself or herself and what other people may think.

Satisfaction or Dissatisfaction

After evaluating the performance of the new car, the purchaser may experience satisfaction or dissatisfaction. For example, if the purchaser ignores inputs that do not agree with expectations, he or she may be satisfied, and the original need (a new car) is fulfilled. A fulfilled (satisfied) need is no longer a motivator because there is no longer tension or desire (need) present.

Reevaulate the Alternatives

If the performance evaluation process results in dissatisfaction, the purchaser may again evaluate other cars that will satisfy his or her need. Thus the state of dissatisfaction results in tension, which may still be a motivator of behavior. Whether or not the person purchases another car will depend on the strength of that need and other needs at that time.

Exercise 5.1: Work Motivation Basics

After exposing you to a very brief overview of motivation, we now want you to analyze your personal views about motivation. Read each statement carefully and indicate your degree of agreement or disagreement with each statement. During the next 10 minutes place on X on the line that best expresses your basic views of work motivation. Check only one answer for each statement.

	(a) Strongly Agree	(b) Agree	(c) Disagree	(d) Strongly Disagree
1 Being nice to people, such as complimenting them on manners or on dress, makes them feel good and is one of the *best* ways to motivate them to work.	_____	_____	_____	_____
2 Coffee breaks and luncheon gatherings of fellow employees help raise morale and are two fairly simple but good means of motivating employees.	_____	_____	_____	_____
3 Giving employees continuing opportunities to test their knowledge and to try their abilities is the strongest factor in motivation.	_____	_____	_____	_____
4 Employees are interested in the paycheck and are generally not too interested in exerting extra effort for other reasons.	_____	_____	_____	_____
5 Lack of motivating factors in a job will force even the well-motivated individual to be more concerned with the surrounding of the job (parking, furniture, etc.).	_____	_____	_____	_____

		(a) Strongly Agree	(b) Agree	(c) Disagree	(d) Strongly Disagree
6	Providing employees with information on the dollar value of their fringe benefits helps them more fully appreciate their jobs and should also help them realize greater job satisfaction.	_____	_____	_____	_____
7	Employees on routine jobs can be motivated through supervisory recognition of their *continual diligence* and *loyalty*.	_____	_____	_____	_____
8	When employees find no satisfaction in a work situation, it may be a place to consider automation.	_____	_____	_____	_____
9	Strict controls, while more expensive, ensure better results than when individuals are made more responsible and have fewer restrictions imposed upon them.	_____	_____	_____	_____
10	An experienced employee who performs well may find all tasks in his/her unit to be routine and a chore. Through periodic rotation from task to task within the unit for variety, his/her work motivation will be maintained.	_____	_____	_____	_____

If you are in a class or seminar, separate into groups of 6 to 10 people each and arrive at a consensus answer for each question.

When your group reaches the point where each person can say, "Well, even though it may not be exactly what I want, at least I can live with the decision and support it," then the group has reached consensus. This doesn't mean that all of the group must completely agree. But all of the group must at least minimally agree. Consequently any one of the group can block a decision. This is precisely why consensus decisions are both more difficult and more effective than other group decision methods, such as voting. It forces the group to consider all aspects of the problem and objections to possible courses of action. Treat differences of opinion as a way of (1) gathering additional information, (2) clarifying issues, and (3) forcing the group to seek better alternatives. Your group has 40 minutes to reach a consensus. After arriving at a group consensus, elect a spokesperson to present the group solution to the other groups. Further learning can be achieved through the exchange of viewpoints between groups.

Answers to Exercise 5.1

| 1 | (d) | 2 | (d) | 3 | (a) | 4 | (d) | 5 | (a) |
| 6 | (d) | 7 | (d) | 8 | (a) | 9 | (d) | 10 | (d) |

Don't get too excited if you disagree with the experts. The answers are based on Herzberg's two-factor theory. It is not critical if you answered a question (b) when the correct answer is (a). What is important is that your answer is on the correct side of the scale. Stated another way, it does not matter if you answered question 1 (c) or (d)—just so you were on the right half of the scale. If you have an incorrect answer and a review of Herzberg's theory does not clarify the issue for you, we suggest that you check with a classmate who answered the question correctly.

Theories of Motivation

After our discussion of the word "motivation," we now will introduce theories of motivation that can serve DP managers as models when motivating subordinates, bosses, or even themselves. The two basic categories of motivation theory are "process" and "content."

Process theories describe motivation as a process or flow of interrelated activities. Figure 5.1 is an example of a process. It may be helpful for the supervisor to remember the process of motivation is similar to the flow of oil through a refinery. The entire process of a refinery can be described in terms of the flow of the oil from raw inputs through refined gas and oil. Process theories attempt to explain motivation from need awareness to satisfaction.

Content theories are theories that describe motivation at a single point in time. If a DP manager could take a snapshot of an employee's behavior, thereby stopping action, the analysis of that photograph is what we mean by content theory. Of course, in actual organizations it is impossible to stop all action and analyze the content of motivating people. However, managers can improve their knowledge of human behavior by having a basic understanding of what motivates employees at any specific time.

There are far more theories of motivation than are discussed here. For purposes of simplification we present.

Figure 5-3   Motivation Outline

Process theories:
     Stimulus-response theory (Skinner)
     Equity theory (Homans, Adams)
     Job characteristics theory (Hackman/Oldmam)
Content theories:
     Need theory (Maslow)
     Motivation-hygiene theory (Herzberg)

---

only the major theories of process and content. Our objective is to present the theories in a straightforward manner that will encourage you to remember the overall points of a few theories that have meaning and application in DP organizations.

Stimulus-Response Theory

Stimulus-response (S-R) theorists argue that behavior can best be understood by studying the relationship between stimuli and responses. They define stimuli as events or activities (internal or external) that modify behavior. They further believe that future responses (new behavior) depend on how a person is reinforced for the new response. The leading American psychologist who has been influential in applying the principles of reinforcement is B. F. Skinner. The best known example of his theory that results determine future behavior is the utopian society he designed in his novel *Walden Two*. In this society, people are placed on contingency reinforcement schedules: desired behavior is rewarded and undesired behavior is punished.

S-R theory has a potential benefit to managers because they are basically interested in when to reward and when to discipline people. The natural question is "Which is more effective—a reward-centered or a punishment-centered manager?"* Figure 5.4 is a diagram of the situation where we introduce two managers to the organization—one is a rewarding manager and one is a punitive manger. The punitive manager has a more positive effect on production in the short run; however, the rewarding manager has a stronger positive effect in the

---

*We do not mean to imply that a manager uses only one style. Rather, we are talking about the dominant style of the manager.

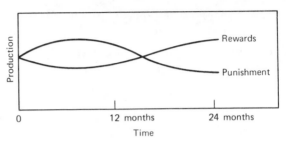

Figure 5-4 Relationship Between Production, Time, and Rein-forcement

long run. The punitive manager increases production in the short run at the expense of the employees. In the long run, subordinates leave the punitive organization or else remain and contribute the minimum effort possible so that they do not attract attention to themselves. Subordinates are simply less committed to the goals of a punitive manager and organization.

When the rewarding manager is introduced into the organization, employees' productivity may take a slight "dip" because the subordinates may be unsure of the style and wonder if the new manager is "for real." After a period of adjustment, productivity under the rewarding manager will exceed productivity under a punitive manager, because employees sense that the rewarding supervisor really is concerned about the task and social relationships. The consequences usually are higher organizational commitment, higher satisfaction, lower turnover, and increased productivity.

If rewarding employees is more effective than punishing them, then why is punishment so frequently used? First, punishment is easy to apply—managers don't have to be creative and think. To use rewards effectively, managers *must* think and put forth that little extra effort to be creative. Second, managers may be rewarded for using punishment because they usually see a quick suppression of undesired behavior and they assume that they have

been effective. Again—remember the long-run consequences of punishment:

1 It will increase anxiety and tension, which normally
   will reduce productivity and satisfaction.

2 Over time the level of punishment must be increased
   by the manager to maintain the continued suppression
   of undesired behavior. Managers soon run out of
   punishment options.

3 Punishment does not get rid of the inappropriate behavior; it merely suppresses it.

4 Mild or light punishment may actually reward certain
   subordinates and increase the rate of inappropriate
   behavior. For some employees, negative feedback is
   better than no feedback. Many people simply desire
   attention.

5 In the long run, productivity that is maintained by force
   will decrease and human resources will be depleted
   because the good people may leave the firm.

Although there are numerous negative effects from the
use of punishment, there are times when a manager may
want to consider the use of punishment. However, we
believe that in any organization only about 5 percent, or
less, of the employees need a "kick in the pants" once in a
while. The other 95 percent of the employees want to do
well and will do well if they are given meaningful work and
leadership. Don't design a punitive control system for all
employees when only a small percentage actually needs
negative motivation. If a manager must use punishment,
the following simple guidelines may be helpful:

1 After the first offense, warn the employee and clearly
   specify what the punishment will be for future viola-
   tions of policy or rules.

2 Don't threaten a subordinate with punishment if you are not willing to follow through and actually punish.

3 Don't let your anger control the counseling session. Be calm and factual. Ask if the employee understands the consequences of repeating the undesired behavior.

4 Punishment should follow the undesired behavior as soon as possible. If you must administer punishment at a later date, "recreate the crime" by verbally linking the punishment to the undesired behavior.

5 Don't keep warning employees; sooner or later you must punish them for undesired behavior. Warn once or twice and then punish.

6 The punishment must be strong enough to stop the inappropriate behavior. Mild punishment may be seen as a reward by certain people and actually increase the inappropriate behavior.

Equity Theory

This theory is very important to supervisors because it helps them understand the thinking of their subordinates and peers when supervisors are thinking about the allocation of rewards and merit increases in organizations. Specifically, equity theory gives the supervisor a feeling for how employees evaluate salaries and merit increases. This theory is especially helpful to DP managers during our current problems with inflation and employee turnover.

Equity is always subjective and relative, and it involves more than one person. First an employee is hired into the organization based on a ratio of outputs to inputs which can be diagrammed as O_a / I_a. Inputs are experience, education, age, skills, seniority, and sex. Outputs include salary, recognition, opportunity for achievement, risk or danger, and boredom. For DP employees to feel equitably treated in the organization, this formula must be roughly in balance. A reminder—this relationship is very subjective and hard to measure! Now, even if this relationship is in balance, employees do not stop searching for information at this point. According to George C. Homans, a noted sociologist, they compare themselves to some other person or group (social reference group) and evaluate the equity of that comparison:

$$\frac{O_a}{I_a} = \frac{O_b}{I_b}$$

where b may be a person or a DP group on or off the job. For example, a systems analyst at the Hartford Insurance may compare herself to another worker at the Hartford or she may compare her job to a like job at Aetna Insurance Company. Homans' suggestion that distributive justice is equitable when the ratio of outputs to inputs of person a is equal to the ratio of outputs to inputs of person b. Research evidence indicates that workers within groups, through informal sanctions, try to keep outputs in line with inputs. This is why the "rate buster" can be an outcast in the informal group. The personnel department, through the process of job evaluation, tries to measure inputs and keep them in line with outputs. Further, the personnel department should compare salaries of DP company employees with comparable jobs in the community, the state, and the nation.* DP managers can be certain that employees and union representatives are making these comparisons.

---

*We attempted to make these comparisons when we surveyed over 700 DP personnel. See J. Daniel Couger and Robert A. Zawacki, "Compensation Preferences of DP Professionals," *Datamation,* November 1978, pp. 96–102.

Job Characteristics Theory

As mentioned earlier, this model identifies five important characteristics of a job (called "core job dimensions"). Skill variety (tasks that challenge the individual's skills and abilities), task identity (completing a "whole" and identifiable piece of work), and task significance (how important is the job to the organization) lead to *experienced meaningfulness of the job*. Task autonomy leads to *experienced responsibility for outcomes* of the job. Finally, feedback concerning effectiveness of the employee's efforts provides *knowledge of results* of the job.

These three "critical psychological states" are associated with high levels of internal motivation, satisfaction, and quality of performance—and with correspondingly low levels of absenteeism and job turnover.

The relationships between the three psychological states listed above and the on-the-job outcomes is illustrated in Figure 2.1. When all three are high, then internal work motivation, job satisfaction, and work quality should be high, and absenteeism and turnover should be low.

Also, using the model, a single index can be computed which characterizes a job's motivating potential. That index is called the "motivating potential score," and can be used to compare DP jobs with other jobs.

We expect that people who have high need for personal growth and development will respond more positively to a job high in motivating potential than will people with low growth need strength.

Obviously, not everyone is able to become internally motivated—even when the motivating potential of the job is high. Behavioral research has shown that the psychological needs of people determine who can (and cannot) become internally motivated at work. Some people have strong need for personal accomplishment—for learning and developing beyond where they are now, for being stimulated and challenged. These people are high in GNS.

The lack of challenge and the low motivating potential of many jobs, as currently constituted in our society, demand careful consideration of work redesign by managers for both humanitarian and productivity reasons. Appendix IV presents our recommended procedures for work redesign.

Content-Based Theories

As indicated earlier, the foregoing theories are labeled process theories because they describe the entire flow of events in the motivating process. We next discuss two major theories that describe what motivates people at a specific point in time content theory.

Need Theory

What is it about a job that motivates workers to produce? Is it money? Supervisors, psychologists, and managers have long debated the relationship between money and productivity. Recently comedian Jackie Mason clarified the argument by stating:

> Some people think the most mportant thing in life is money. It's not true. Love is the most important thing in life. Personally, I'm very fortunate because I love money.

Although this statement was made in a humorous way, we recognize that very few people would work if they were not paid for it. Abraham Maslow was one of the first people to recognize the relationship between money and people's other needs. He did this by developing a hierarchy of needs (see Figure 5.5).

Maslow established that workers are motivated by different needs at different times and workers needs are in a rough hierarchy from lower order needs to higher order needs. He reasoned that workers have a primary need for food and shelter; after that need is met, workers become interested in their financial security, then social needs, then esteem needs, and finally self-fulfillment needs. Tragic evidence of this hierarchy of needs came to the authors' attention recently in Colorado. When the Big Thompson Canyon flooded in the summer of 1976, many of the survivors of that tragedy probably were going through life at the social or esteem level of needs before the flood. After the 30-foot wall of water came down that narrow canyon and destroyed almost all of their homes, their needs were immediately reduced to the basic level—food and shelter. Managers should evaluate where their workers are on Maslow's hierarchy of needs and adjust

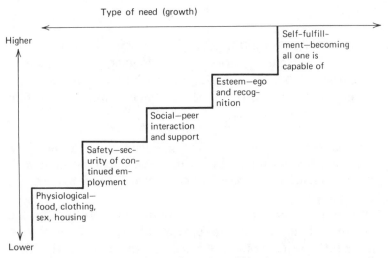

Figure 5-5 Hierarchy of Needs

rewards accordingly. Some important points to remember are:

1 To be effective, a motivator must be perceived by the *subordinate* as a motivator.

2 One hundred percent of the workers' needs do not have to be met before they begin to look for the higher order needs: 95 percent of their physiological needs may be met, 80 percent of their security needs, and only 20 percent of their social needs.

3 A satisfied need is not a motivator of behavior.

4 The lower order needs are met by and large by society, a private corporation, public agency, or even a welfare program.

5 While money is important as a motivator, other needs should be considered such as the meaningfulness of the job itself.

6 Lower level needs must be satisfied before the higher level needs become motivators. Young workers may place a higher priority on lower needs such as salaries when they are starting their families and purchasing homes.

7 Very few people in our society are operating at the self-fulfillment level; however, many people are striving toward this ultimate goal.

8 A worker's position on the hierarchy of needs may change with the time and situation—a person can move in two directions.

9 DP professionals (analysts and programmers) have the highest need for self-fulfillment and growth (GNS) of any job category or profession for which we have data.

10 DP professionals have a lower social need (4.20) than the average score for other professionals (5.48). This

low social need must be recognized when we promote the best DP analyst to be the systems manager. The new job requires mostly people skills and may require training that emphasizes organizational behavior skills.

11 DP operations (computer operators and data control personnel), although not as high as DP professionals, still have an above-average GNS when compared to the population in general. This means that they need meaningful jobs that provide challenge and the opportunity to grow on the job.

12 DP operations personnel have significantly higher social needs than DP professionals. Therefore, operations personnel may be more receptive to assuming management positions and functions such as attending staff meetings, coordination, and negotiation.

Motivation-Hygiene Theory

A second content theory of motivation, presented in the 1950s by Frederick Herzberg, has become known as the two-factor approach. Herzberg was the first person to say that dissatisfaction and satisfaction are not the endpoints of a continuous line. They are, in fact, two separate scales (see Figure 5.6).

Without certain things at the place of work, Herzberg maintained, workers will be dissatisfied. And if a supervisor meets only the workers' maintenance needs, they will *not* be satisfied—they will only be *not dissatisfied* or not unhappy. To be happy or satisfied, workers basically need jobs that have motivational characteristics or satisfiers.

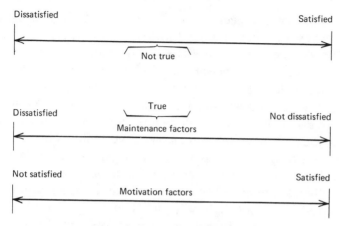

Figure 5-6   Satisfaction and Dissatisfaction

Note that without the maintenance factors, workers will be unhappy. But given the maintenance factors they will not be happy. To motivate people to increase productivity DP managers must examine the satisfiers of a job after meeting employees' maintenance needs. Further note that the maintenance factors are concerned with the surroundings of the job (extrinsic or external) and the

Dissatisfiers— Maintenance Factors	Satisfiers— Motivation Factors
Company policy and administration	Achievement
Work conditions	Recognition
Technical supervision	Advancement and growth
Interpersonal relations with peers	Responsibility
Job security	The work itself
Pay	

Figure 5-7   Maintenance Factors and Motivation Factors

motivators are concerned with the job itself and how employees feel about the job (intrinsic or internal).*

Pay is listed as a dissatisfier, and this may puzzle the reader because all people are willing to accept more pay—we will not turn down a pay increase. Herzberg listed pay as a dissatisfier because his industrial research indicated that when salary schedules are perceived by the employees as inequitable their negative feelings are three times as strong as when pay is considered equitable. When such imbalance occurs, employees are *very* unhappy. Nevertheless, even when salary schedules are equitable, employees are only slightly happy. Herzberg recommends that managers simply get greater returns on effort and investment by concentrating on the satisfiers. # The following exercise is designed to help the reader review the two-factor theory and attempt to make practical applications of the theory. We normally find that DP personnel are very creative and pleasantly surprised with their outcomes in this exercise.

Exercise 5.2 Enrichment Exercise

Divide the class or workshop into groups of six to ten people and brainstorm ways to enrich the following job. Each group should make a list of ways to enrich this job

---

*We are not saying that managers should not provide the maintenance factors. Rather, DP managers must provide a sufficient foundation of maintenance factors that meets the competition for your employees. Only the DP manager (with the help of personnel) can determine what are equitable maintenance factors.

#The reader should be warned that Herzberg did his research in the early 1950s, when yearly inflation was very low. During the present period of high inflation salary is on everyone's mind because money takes on other meanings in our society such as status, recognition, and the means of at least maintaining standards of living with ever-increasing living costs.

without placing a value on the individual suggestion. In a brainstorning session, any input is solicited and encouraged. Appoint a spokesperson to report the results of the brainstorming session to the other groups. The group has 40 minutes to brainstorn.

* The job to enrich is that of janitor.
* There are 150 janitors.
* There are nine supervisors.
* They work in a large central Canadian city cleaning subways.
* There are three shifts.
* There is no union.
* The yearly salary range for janitors is $7,200 to $10,200. This is a very competitive salary in this city.
* Yearly increases are based on seniority, not merit.
* Supplies and uniforms are purchased by the city's purchasing department.
* The citizens of this metropolitan city are constantly complaining to city hall about dirty subways.
* The nine supervisors are the people who have been janitors for the longest period of time.
* The city council employs your group as consultants to improve the situation.

After completing Exercise 5.2 and being introduced to Maslow's and Herzberg's content theories of motivation, it is logical to be concerned about the relation between the two theories. Basically, the two theories support each other (see Figure 5.8). The lower order of needs in Maslow's hierarchy is roughly equivalent to Herzberg's maintenance factors, and Maslow's higher order of needs parallels Herzberg's motivators. Both theories are excellent models for helping DP managers determine what will be motivational for each employee.

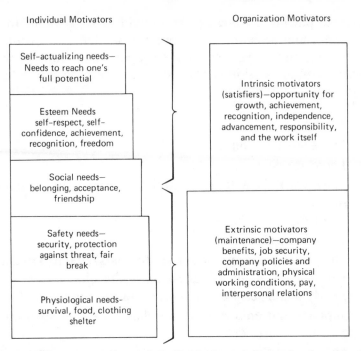

Individual Motivators   Organization Motivators

Figure 5-8 Interaction of Individual and Organization Motivators

Answers to Exercise 5.2

There are no correct answers to the brainstorming exercise. Please review the guidelines for work redesign in Appendix IV.

Summary

Motivation is a series of events that begins with a felt need (tension), involves a search process, action (selection), evaluation, and a reassessment of the need. Human behavior is caused, goal-directed, and motivated.

There are process and content theories of motivation. The three main process theories are stimulus-response, equity, and job characteristics theory. The two main content theories are need and motivation-hygiene. Process theories describe motivation as a process or flow of interrelated events, whereas content theories describe motivation at a single point in time.

The punishment-centered manager has a dramatic (positive) effect on production in the short run; however, the reward-centered manager is more effective in the long run. In the long run, subordinates will leave the punitive organization if they have that option. If they cannot leave, they may put forward less than maximum effort because of lack of commitment to the manager and organization.

Frederick Herzberg introduced the idea that dissatisfaction and satisfaction are not the ends of a continuous line. He emphasized that there are indeed two lines, maintenance factors and motivation factors. The maintenance (hygiene) factors are (1) company policy and administration, (2) work conditions, (3) technical supervision, (4) interpersonal relations with peers, (5) job security, and (6) pay. The motivators are (1) achievement, (2) recognition, (3) advancement and growth, (4) responsibility, and (5) the work itself. The maintenance factors are concerned with the surroundings of the job (extrinsic) and the motivators are concerned with the job itself and how employees feel about the job (intrinsic). Pay is the most controversial of the factors because of the many meanings attached to pay. Further, in periods of inflation, almost everyone is concerned about pay.

Job characteristics theory is an extension of Herzberg's two-factor theory because it divides the work itself into five core job dimensions. The five core job dimensions are skill variety, task identity, task significance, autonomy, and feedback from the job. The presence of these five core job dimensions lead to critical psychological states, which in turn lead to higher personal and work outcomes. This motivation process is moderated by the employees' GNS, which is the workers' need to grow and develop on the job.

Our national surveys of DP organizations indicate that feedback is a problem in most organizations. Chapter 6 contains guidelines for DP managers on planning, joint goalsetting, and feedback.

Notes

1 Harold J. Leavitt, *Managerial Psychology* (Chicago: University of Chicago Press, 1964), p. 12.
2 *Prevention,* August 1975, p. 1.
3 Leon Festinger, *A Theory of Cognitive Dissonance* (Stanford: Stanford University Press, 1957).

Bibliography

Carrell, M. R., and J. E. Dittrich. "Employee Perceptions of Fair Treatment," *Personnel Journal,* October 1976, pp. 523–524.

Couger, J. Daniel, and Robert A. Zawacki. "What Motivates DP Professionals?" *Datamation,* September 1978, pp. 116–123.

French, Wendell L., Cecil H. Bell, Jr., and Robert A. Zawacki. *Organization Development: Theory, Practice and Research.* Dallas: Business Publications, 1978.

Gellerman, S. W. *The Management of Human Resources.* Hinsdale, Ill: Dryden Press, 1976.

Herzberg, Frederick. "The Motivation-Hygiene Concept and

Problems of Manpower," in *Organization Development: Managing Change in the Public Sector*, Robert A. Zawacki and D. D. Warrick, eds. Chicago: IPMA, 1976, pp. 178–182.

Maslow, A. H. "The Need for Creative People," in *Organization Development: Managing Change in the Public Sector*, Robert A. Zawacki and D. D. Warrick, eds. Chicago: IPMA, 1976, pp. 206–209.

Maslow, Abraham. *Motivation and Personality*. New York: Harper & Row, 1954.

McClelland, D. C., and D. G. Winter. *Motivating Economic Achievement*. New York: Free Press, 1969.

McGregor, D. *The Human Side of Enterprise*. New York: McGraw-Hill, 1960.

Porter, Lyman W., and Edward E. Lawler, III. "What Job Attitudes Tell About Motivation," *Harvard Business Review*, Vol. 46, January–February, 1968, pp. 118–126.

Reif, William E. "Intrinsic versus Extrinsic Rewards: Resolving the Controversy," *Human Resources Management*, Vol. 14, Summer 1975, pp. 2–10.

Roberts, Karlene H., and Frederick Savage. "Twenty Questions Utilizing Job Satisfaction Measures," *California Management Review*, Vol. 15, Summer 1973, pp. 21–28.

Rosenbach, William E., Robert A. Zawacki, and Cyril P. Morgan. "Research Round-up," *The Personnel Administrator*, October 1977, pp. 51–61.

Scanlan, B. K. "Determinates of Job Satisfaction and Productivity," *Personnel Journal*, January 1976, pp. 12–14.

Terkel, Studs. *Working*. New York: Avon Books, 1974.

Vroom, V. H. *Work and Motivation*. New York: Wiley, 1964.

6

PLANNING, JOINT
GOALSETTING, AND FEEDBACK

Our national study of DP managers indicates that they
perceive supervisory feedback as needing improvement.
So do their subordinates. Our studies also revealed both
low social need strength (SNS) and high growth need
strength (GNS) of DP managers compared to other managers in organizations. The combination of these need
characteristics may inhibit effective feedback, both with
subordinates and with other managers. Once recognized,
the negative aspects of these characteristics may be coun-
teracted, with application of some of the planning, joint
goalsetting, and feedback techniques discussed in this
chapter.

To accomplish DP work, there must be an understanding of what is to be done and planning what is to be done is
the primary function of DP managers. However, before we
discuss planning, some basic definitions are in order.

- **Planning** This is the process whereby we anticipate
  the future and determine what steps are necessary to
  achieve the organization's desired results. Thus plan-

ning involves two basic dimensions: (1) assessing the future and (2) providing the people and monies to achieve the desired outcome.

* **Objectives** They are the goals that a supervisor wishes to accomplish. An example of an objective is "To increase the output of Team Project C 10 percent this calendar year."

* **Policies** Policies are broad, general statements of a company's objectives. For example, a common policy in a DP organization may be "Each employee is permitted to take 21 days of annual paid vacation each year."

* **Rules** Rules are very specific statements indicating how supervisors implement policies and objectives. An example of a rule is: "Employees must apply for annual paid vacation at least 30 working days prior to the effective date of the vacation."

You probably have assumed correctly by now that, of all the management functions, planning must be first. Further, it can be either personal or organizational. It can be short range, intermediate range, or long range. It can be formal or informal.

The breakout of the planning process in Figure 6.1 can be helpful to DP managers for several reasons. First, when managers fail, one of the primary reasons is that they *plan to fail*. By this we mean that they usually fail to plan for the future. Usually they do not plan for the future because they believe that they do not have ample time or information needed to plan. Most DP managers are so busy putting out "brushfires" that they firmly believe planning is a luxury. We call this situation "getting seduced by the daily task at the expense of planning." While managers cannot ignore the immediate daily problems, they should recognize that proper planning is the key to effective management and they must reserve some time during the

Time

Type	Short Range (1 year)	Intermediate (2-5 years)	Long Range (5 years +)
Personal			
Group or project			
Organization			

Figure 6-1 Planning Chart

week for planning. The American Management Association recommends that supervisors divide their day according to the following guidelines (recognize that these are only guidelines and deviations are necessary and expected):

- 38 percent on daily problems (crises supervision and routine decisions).
- 40 percent on problems and deadlines within one week.
- 15 percent on problems and deadlines within one month.
- 5 percent on problems and deadlines within three to six months.
- 2 percent on problems and deadlines one year or more away.

Notice that the largest percentage of a DP manager's time should be used for daily and/or weekly problems and deadlines. Intermediate and long-range planning consume a very small percentage of a manager's time; however, the long-range implications of planning should not be ignored.

After recognizing the importance of planning, new managers usually get mentally "overloaded" because they fail to distinguish personal goals from group and organizational goals. For example, we have found it helpful to ask new managers to design a personal plan of what they want to accomplish during the next year and by the end of five years. Then we ask them to identify how they can accomplish some of their personal goals by participating in the work group's and organization's goals. This exercise encourages managers to plan for the future both in personal and organizational terms. Linking personal and organizational goals is a healthy process and a process that is missing in some organizations.

The Planning Process

As previously stated, the planning process can be either formal or informal. The degree to which managers formalize plans will depend on the importance of their plans and the amount of time and effort they want to invest. Whether and to what degree to formalize a plan is a very subjective decision. However, if a manager is going to err, we recommend erring on the side of formalizing.

Preston P. LeBreton, past president of the Academy of Management and professor of business administration at the University of Washington, has developed a formal planning process.* LeBreton was a major influence on one of the authors of this book, and therefore on the following guidelines. Please note that the following planning guidelines refer only to *what* must be done. We do not specify *how* to accomplish the tasks—that will be discussed later in this chapter in the section on joint goalsetting.

---

*Many of these planning ideas came from informal class notes taken from lectures by Professor LeBreton. Other ideas appear in Preston B. LeBreton, *General Administration: Planning and Implementation* (New York: Holt, Rinehart & Winston, 1965).

- Become aware of the need to plan.

  Are there multiple sources of input—internal or external?

  Financial, people, or information idea?

- Form an exact statement of the objective of the proposal.

  Formal or informal?

  Who will write the statement?

  What is the nature of the objective?

- Prepare a general outline of the proposal.

  What is the nature of the plan?

  What resources are needed?

  What supporting evidence is there?

  What is the time schedule?

  Who is responsible for its implementation?

- Obtain approval of the proposal.

  Who will make the presentation?

  To whom and in what format?

  Where and when?

- Organize planning functions and assign responsibility.

  What people will be involved?

  Does plan cross departments or divisions?

  Who will notify people about the need to plan this action?

- Consider contacts with cooperating departments and divisions.

  Who will make the contact?

  Who will they contact?

  Formal or informal notification?

  When will they be contacted?

- Obtain and evaluate inputs.

  What inputs do we need?

  How will they be obtained?

  Who has the information?

What format shall we use?
How are the data evaluated?

- Form tentative conclusions and prepare a tentative plan.

    How does the plan compare with original objective?
    What is the probability that the planned-for events will happen?
    Is the final solution practical?
    Have we considered all of the alternatives?

- Test the tentative plan.

    Formal or informal testing?
    What parts are to be tested?
    By whom?
    What type of tests?

- Prepare the final plan.

    Time schedule?
    Who?
    Resources needed?
    Budget needed?
    Is the supporting evidence included?

- Obtain approval of the final plan.

    Who makes the presentation?
    Who approves the plan?
    Who communicates the final plan?
    To whom is the final plan communicated?
    Who follows up on the implementation (action) phases?
    When will progress reports be due?

Joint Goal Setting

Plans and objectives can be determined automatically or in a collaborative manner. One collaborative process of es-

Project	Project Leader	Team Members	Date Started	Draft of Plan Due	Budget	Completion Date
1.						
2.						
3.						
4.						
5.						
6.						

Figure 6-2 Planning Chart

tablishing objectives is commonly known as joint goalsetting or management by objectives (MBO).

Obstacles to Effective Goalsetting and Feedback

As indicated in Chapter 4 (figures 4.5 and 4.6), our research shows that DP managers are generally satisfied with the amount of input they have in the goalsetting process; the average rating is 5.5 on the scale of 7. However, they perceive that feedback on goal accomplishment needs considerable improvement. General feedback is rated even lower. The magnitude of the problem is inversely proportional to the management level; the lower the level of the DP manager, the greater the problem.

Figure 6.3 shows that feedback ratings for both DP managers and their employees is lower than that of their peers in other parts of the company.

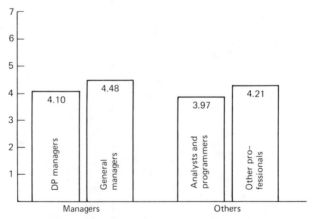

Figure 6-3   Feedback from Management

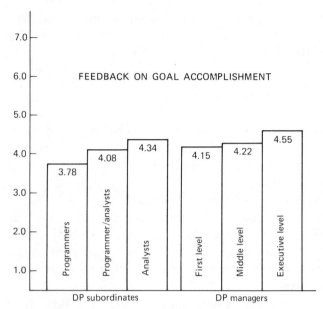

Figure 6-4   Feedback on Goal Accomplishment

The Hackman/Oldham survey did not include questions on goalsetting and feedback. Figure 6.4 shows only the comparison of DP management to subordinates. Both managers and subordinates perceive the need for improvement in feedback.

The feedback problem, perceived at all levels of the organization, may also be caused by the unique SNS characteristics of personnel in the computer field.

SNS for DP managers is only 4.51, two-thirds that of peers in other parts of the company. In this characteristic, DP managers are more like their subordinates than their peers. SNS for analysts and programmers averages 4.20.

Since supervisors are frequently promoted from the programming and analysis ranks, it is not surprising that their SNS is low.

Implications for Feedback

People with low social needs can be expected to interact less with subordinates. Communication skill may not come naturally for such people. In contrast, people with high SNS frequently gravitate to fields such as sales, where a great deal of interaction is required.

As discussed in Chapter 2, the entry level job for the DP field requires less interaction than the majority of jobs in the typical firm. People can succeed as computer programmers with a low degree of interaction compared to other jobs.

Nevertheless, a person can acquire the skills for effective communication. The following measures are recommended:

1   People who do not inherently possess communication skills can acquire them through formal training. Acquiring knowledge about behavioral concepts and skills concerning communications techniques can offset the negative effects of low social need.

2   When feedback is not produced naturally—because of low SNS—more formalized feedback procedures are needed. Training in effective feedback approaches can improve application of the procedure.

3   Because DP personnel are frequently promoted to management based primarily on technical competence, they need formal training in the behavioral areas. Because DP personnel have unique characteristics in GNS and SNS, supervisory and management development workshops should be designed by personnel with

DP backgrounds and coordinated with experts in organizational behavior.

4   Personnel designing these workshops must remember that feedback skills for DP managers (or future managers) are harder to develop because of a lack of an adequate role model within DP management. Thus DP managerial career path training needs to place strong emphasis on feedback skills—both in giving and receiving feedback. Appendix III of this book contains guidelines on giving and receiving feedback.

A recent study by Zawacki and Taylor of the top industrial organizations in the United States indicates that approximately 55 percent of U.S. firms are using a form of joint goalsetting. Another recent study[2] indicates that 122 out of 147 firms surveyed have a form of joint goalsetting. Further, only 15 percent of the 122 companies stated that they were dissatisfied with their goal setting.

A joint goalsetting program is based on the following concepts:

1   Managing a successful organization or being a successful person in one's job does not have to be a matter of luck or of letting events shape one's life or organization.

2   Organizations or people with goals have a greater chance of making things happen and building a successful growth pattern than those who simply watch things happen, criticize what happened, wonder what happened, or wait for fate to mold their organization or their lives.

What Is Joint Goalsetting?

Joint goalsetting is a management method and process where *objectives* (the word *goals* may be used to mean the

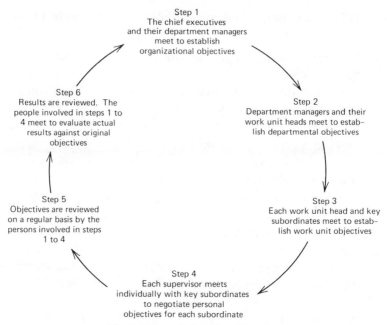

Figure 6-5   Joint Goal Setting

same thing as *objectives* in this context) are established for
(1) the DP organization, (2) each department, (3) each
work unit within each department, and (4) each employee
who works in an area where the establishment of objectives would be practical and valuable. Establishing objectives usually consists of having the key people affected by
the objectives meet to (1) agree on the major objectives for
a given time period such as one year, (2) develop plans for
how and when the objectives will be accomplished, and (3)
decide on the criteria for determining if the objectives have
been met. Once objectives have been established, progress
reviews are made regularly until the period for which the
objectives are established is over. At that time the people
who established the objectives at each level in the organi-

zation meet to evaluate actual results with the established objectives and then agree on the objectives for the next period (see Figure 6.5). As a philosophy of management, joint goalsetting is bound on five assumptions:

1　. . . assumes that people are willing to commit themselves to goals in which they participate.

2　. . . assumes that people will perform better if they can measure their progress.

3　. . . assumes that people are achievement and goal oriented and will make a contribution to the organization if they are given the opportunity to do so. This is especially true for DP personnel with their high GNS.

4　. . . emphasizes results rather than means.

5　. . . assumes that people perform better when they have some say in their destiny.

Advantages

This procedure is not a panacea and like most worthwhile programs it is not without its problems. However, the following benefits are among those that can accrue from joint goalsetting:

1　Planning is accomplished—looking to the future and not the past.

2　Communications and feedback can be improved.

3　People have a clearer understanding of what is expected of them and how well they are doing and feedback is increased.

4　Greater employee commitment, direction, and teamwork result.

5   The manager-subordinate relationship becomes more of a helping relationship.

6   Duplication of effort is reduced.

7   Needless conflict resulting from unclear goals is reduced.

8   "Busy work" that does not relate to organizational objectives is reduced.

9   A more objective way to evaluate employees and to reward effective employees is set up.

10 Problems in accomplishing goals are forced to the surface, where they can be confronted objectively.

11 Those who wish to participate in the program see that they can have a greater influence in running their organization and shaping their own careers than they had previously allowed for.

12 Many problems are solved before they result in a crisis, so the need for crises management is reduced.

Disadvantages

As with all management technique, joint goalsetting has some disadvantages that the DP manager should recognize. These are:

1   Time and commitment by the supervisor and subordinates are required.

2   It's hard work (points 1 and 2 in the above list may be seen as disadvantages by the employees).

3   The personnel department may take over, with no input by the employees in the various DP departments.

4   It may become overstructured.

5 The supervisor may not be able to link rewards with goal accomplishment.

6 Without top management support, it may fail.

7 Learning and practice by the participants are required.

Guidelines for Writing Objectives

After you have written a goal statement (see Figure 6.6), check it against the criteria presented below. If your goal seems to be poorly written or unclear, you may want to devote more time to improving the way you have stated it.

Well Written Goals Are:	Poorly Written Goals Are:
Stated in terms of end-results.	Stated in terms of process or activities.
Achievable in definite time period.	Never fully achievable; no specific target date.
Definite as to what is expected.	Ambiguous as to what is expected.
Practical and feasible.	Theoretical or idealistic.
Important to the meaningfulness of work.	Of no real consequence.
Precisely stated in terms of quantities, where possible.	Too brief and indefinite, or too long and complex.
Limited to one important goal statement.	Written with two or more goals per statement.
Require stretching of the 5 core job dimensions to improve results.	Follow established policies and procedures.

Goal Level (check the appropriate one):

1. Organization (company-wide)
2. Department (products, etc.)
3. Work unit (Project team, key punching, etc.)
4. Personal

Period _____

Goal Type (check the appropriate one):

1. Routine responsibilities ____
2. Problem solving ____
3. Innovative ____
4. Organizational development ____
5. Personal development ____
6. Other ____

Goal (What do I/we want to accomplish?)	Goal Plan (What must be done to accomplish the goal?)	Goal Completion Target Date (When should the goal be completed?)	How Goal Attainment Will Be Measured (How will I/we know when the goal is accomplished?)

Figure 6-6   Goal Setting Form

Summary

Planning is a primary function of managers. It is a process whereby supervisors anticipate the future and determine the necessary steps to achieve the organization's results. Plans are of three types: personal, group, and organizational. Further, there are short-range, intermediate, and long-range plans.

The planning process can be either formal or informal. The degree to which managers formalize a plan will depend on the importance of the plan to the organization. Plans refer to what must be done. How to accomplish the plan is part of joint goalsetting.

Joint goalsetting is a process where objectives are established for (1) the DP organization, (2) each department, (3) each work unit within each department, and (4) every employee. Usually the key people in the organization meet to (1) agree on the major organizational objectives for the next year, (2) develop plans for how the objectives will be reached, and (3) decide on the criteria for determining if the objectives have been met. Once this process is complete, regular progress reviews are necessary to keep the organization on a course that leads toward goal accomplishment.

Notes

1   Robert A. Zawacki and Robert L. Taylor, "A View of Performance Appraisal from Organizations Using It," *Personnel Journal,* June 1976, pp. 290–299.

2   "EDP Leads the Thirteen Most Popular Management Techniques," *Administrative Management,* June 1973, pp. 26–29 and 64–65.

Bibliography

Carter, Deborah Ann. "The Light at the End of the Productivity Tunnel," *Supervisory Management,* June 1979, pp. 29–34.

French, W. L., and Hollmann, R. W. "Management By Objectives: The Team Approach," *California Management Review,* Vol. 17, Spring 1975, pp. 13–22.

Hollman, Robert W. "Applying MBO Research to Practice," *Human Resources Management,* Vol. 15, Winter 1976, pp. 28–36.

LeBreton, Preston B. *General Administration: Planning and Implementation.* New York: Holt, Rinehart, & Winston, 1965.

Pounds, William F. "The Process of Problem Finding," *Industrial Management Review,* Fall 1969, pp. 1–19.

Taylor, Robert L., and Robert A. Zawacki. "Collaborative Goal Setting in Performance Appraisal: A Field Experiment," *Public Personnel Management,* May-June 1978, pp. 162-170.

Walton, Richard E. "Contrasting Designs for Participative Systems," in *Organization Development: Managing Change in the Public Sector,* Robert A. Zawacki and D. D. Warrick, eds. Chicago: IPMA, 1976, pp. 75–81.

Zawacki, Robert A., and P. E. LaSota. "Successful Staff Meetings," *Personnel Journal,* January 1975, pp. 27–28, 63–64.

7

ENHANCING MOTIVATION
AND PRODUCTIVITY

With the foundation built on information in the preceding chapters, we can begin to discuss approaches to more effectively assign tasks to employees. Assigning tasks that are aligned with the growth need strength (GNS) of individuals enhances motivation and productivity.

The national norms on employee perceptions were the means (averages) of the survey respondents. Standard deviation was low compared to that of other professions in the Hackman/Oldham (H/O) data base. Individuals in our departments are more homogeneous than those in other professions. Nevertheless, in each department there are individual differences. A major objective in productivity improvement is to carefully consider those individual differences in the assignment of tasks. We first examine the characteristics of the task, then analyze the differences in response to task assignment according to the GNS of the individual.

Scope of Task

Some tasks contain a high degree of the five core job demensions: skill variety, task identity, task significance, autonomy, and feedback. An example is system design. Such tasks are called "high-scope" tasks.

Other tasks contain a relatively low degree of the core job dimensions. An example is system documentation. Such tasks are called "low-scope" tasks.

Individual Responses

Individuals vary in their need for growth, for challenging work. Some persons are more satisfied in performing high-scope tasks; others prefer low-scope tasks. The goal in motivating personnel is to match the scope of the task with the growth need of the individual.

Two graphic models[1] will be used to discuss the alignment of task to individual needs. Figure 7.1 provides the first of those graphic models. The four cells portray the possible assignments.

Cell 1   High-Scope Task + High GNS = High-Level Congruence

Individuals in cell 1 have high GNS. They desire tasks that are challenging: complex, nonstructured tasks they perceive as significant. They want a high-scope task for which they feel responsible and are aware of expected performance.[2] If we have a match in scope of task and GNS, we have a high level of congruence between task and indi-

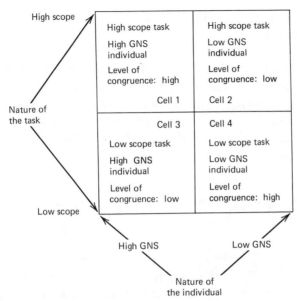

Figure 7.1 Level of Congruence Resulting from Degree of Match Between GNS and Task Scope.

vidual need. An example of a high-scope task is new system development.

Cell 2   High-Scope Task + Low GNS = Low-Level Congruence

Cell 2 reflects the situation where an employee with low GNS is assigned a high-scope task. The level of congruence is low and a poor motivational environment results. An example is a person whose GNS is low being promoted from operations into the system developmental area. One would not expect good productivity in this situation unless other measures are introduced to influence the disparity between task/individual need.

Cell 3   Low-Scope Task + High GNS = Low-Level Congruence

In the situation depicted in cell 3, an employee with high GNS is assigned a low-scope task. The level of congruence is low. The employee is likely to be frustrated and dissatisfied. There is no assurance that the level of productivity will be high. Other measures can be introduced to facilitate productivity, as will be explained below.

Cell 4   Low-Scope Task + Low GNS = High-Level Congruence

The third cell reflects the situation where low GNS employees (like the former computer operator just described) are assigned less demanding tasks, such as program maintenance. A high level of congruence exists between task and individual need. The motivational environment is good and a concomitant level of productivity can be expected.

Imperfection in Task Assignment

The nature of the work in the DP department makes it difficult to perfectly align individuals with the desired scope of task. The high-congruence (cell 1/cell 4) situation can rarely be applied on a continuous basis. In the systems development area, there are many projects to computerize, some challenging, some relatively mundane. In addition, maintenance is occupying an increasing proportion of the systems department budget. The more systems computerized, the more maintenance to perform.

Even with a large backlog of systems to be developed, it is not always possible to assign high-scope work to employees with high GNS. For example on implementation of a system it is often necessary to keep the design team intact to handle the inevitable modifications or corrections during the early months of operation of the system.

Another reason for incongruence exists. With the turnover problem in the industry, it is not infrequent that persons are assigned tasks for which, in a psychological sense, they are underqualified.

In the operations area an entirely different environment exists. For example, there is little correspondence with the level of complexity of a computer operator's job and the degree of complexity of the applications being processed. A huge, complex number-crunching job requires little operator involvement, whereas a simply payroll job requires lots of operator activity in media handling. In the more challenging area of job scheduling there is opportunity for match-up of employees with high GNS. To a much lesser degree this is true in data entry.

Supervisors of operations can utilize job enlargement approaches like job rotation and job enrichment techniques like joint goalsetting. Nevertheless, there are times where cell 2 and cell 3 situations exist, at least for the short run.

Leadership styles can be varied to enhance the motivational environment when situations of low congruence cannot be avoided. The following section explains this approach.

Four Leadership Styles

The behavioral scientists have identified the following four basic styles of leadership.[3,4]

1 *Directive leadership* Characterized by a leader who lets subordinates know what is expected of them, gives

specific guidance as to what should be done and how it should be done, makes his or her part in the group understood, schedules work to be done, maintains definite standards of performance, and asks that group members follow standard rules and regulations.

2 *Supportive leadership* Characterized by a leader who is friendly and approachable, who shows concern for the status, well-being, and needs of subordinates, does things to make the work more pleasant, and treats members as equals.

3 *Participative   and   achievement-oriented   leadership* Characterized by a leader who consults with subordinates, solicits their suggestions, and takes these suggestions into consideration before making a decision. This is a leader who sets challenging goals, expects subordinates to perform at their highest level, continuously seeks improvement in performance, and shows a high degree of confidence that the subordinates will assume responsibility, put forth effort, and accomplish challenging goals.

4 *Maintenance leadership* Characterized by a leader who is available to answer questions when subordinates need guidance and direction. This type of leader does not interfere with the day-to-day tasks. He or she is simply there and maintains the status quo.

Figure 7.2 depicts the way in which leadership style may be varied to increase employee satisfaction and productivity. The recommended leadership style for each cell is described next.

Cell 1 Leadership Style

This situation suggests two types of leader behavior. Achievement-oriented leader behavior is expected to

motivate employees to strive for higher levels of productivity and to have more confidence in their ability to
meet the challenging demands of their job. Further, participative leader behavior would also be appropriate.
Mitchell[5] suggests that such behavior should serve to
clarify organizational contingencies. It should allow subordinates to select goals that are personally meaningful,
allow the subordinate more control over the task, and
facilitate ego involvement on the part of the subordinate.

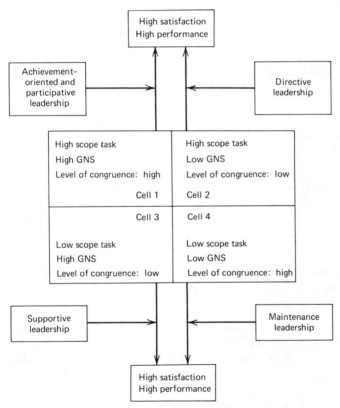

Figure 7.2 Leadership Style Needed to Support Varying Match
on GNS and Task Scope.

Employees with higher-order growth needs would also be internal in orientation and desirous of autonomy and self-control.

Cell 2 Leadership Style

This situation is characterized by individuals who, because of lack of ability or desire, have difficulty coping with this ambiguous situation. As a consequence they would be expected to have difficulty in structuring their own activities. The function of the leader here would appear to be to provide task structure by planning, organizing, coordinating, directing, and controlling the work of subordinates. Such behavior is analogous to directive leadership. It is expected, then, that this form of behavior by the leader in the cell 2 situation would lead to favorable outcomes.[6]

Cell 3 Leadership Style

This situation is characterized by high-GNS employees assigned to low-scope tasks. These individuals will tend to look to their job as one source of need satisfaction but will find these needs unfulfilled because of the nature of their task. Their reaction will probably be frustration and dissatisfaction. The research of House and colleagues suggests that employees who perform this type of frustrating and dissatisfying work will respond favorably to supportive leader behavior.

This form of leader behavior focuses on the leader being friendly and approachable and exhibiting concern for the well-being of subordinates. This supportive behavior will probably not eliminate feelings of frustration and dissatisfaction; however, the dysfunctional consequences of these feelings can, perhaps, be minimized.

Cell 4 Leadership

In this situation a low-scope task is being performed by an employee with low GNS. The level of individual-task congruence is high. Directive leader behavior will probably be inappropriate since the employee will not need the job structured. Similarly, supportive behavior will also be unnecessary, since the employee is not likely to be frustrated or dissatisfied. Participative and achievement-oriented leader behaviors are advocated when the employee is ego involved with the task and is deriving intrinsic satisfaction from it. Since these characteristics are not descriptive of the cell 4 situation, these forms of leader behavior would be inappropriate. What is more appropriate is a form of minimum-interference leader behavior, whereby the leader monitors performance but doesn't actively supervise the employee.[7] Little or no interaction between the leader and subordinate would be required as long as adequate levels of performance are maintained. Hence this form of behavior might be termed maintenance leader behavior. This does not mean, however, that no supervision is required. Rather, the leader in this situation may find it appropriate to maintain a low level of involvement with her or his subordinates. If performance and/or satisfaction problems arise, the leader may, however, intervene in a directive and/or supportive fashion to deal with the problem. Once the deficiency has been corrected, the supervisor reverts back to maintenance leadership.

Introducing Change

Based on the results of the national surveys, some new information is available for management of data processing. Will it be treated merely as interesting information or will it be used to introduce some improvements in the motivational environment of the organization? It may be helpful to examine a general model which conceptualizes the process of change.

The model originated from the studies of psychologist Edgar Schein, who carried out an extensive study of Communist brainwashing techniques used during the Korean War.[8] From this experience, Schein developed a "model" that can be used in thinking about the steps essential to implementing behavioral change. Although this model was developed using many examples of coercion, it can also be used by those wishing to direct changes in their own behavior or changes in the behavior of others through cooperative effort.

One of the cases studied by Schein will serve as a basis for identifying the major parts in his approach. In this particular example Schein examined the procedure used in trying to brainwash a Catholic priest who had been taken captive as a prisoner of war. The procedure followed in this brainwashing involved a three-step process. The first step was to place the priest into a cell with several other people who were stooges. These stooges would point out any time that the priest bothered them. They tried to show him that his self-concept was incorrect. They wanted to convince him that instead of being a help to people, as he had always thought always thought of himself, he was a bother to them.

The second step in this process was to continually interrogate the priest. He was pressured to make a confession. However, his interrogators would not tell him what to confess because they wanted the change to be his own. After several months the priest finally began to write his own confessions.

The third step in the process occurred when the priest had begun writing confessions. He was again placed with a group of stooges and they showed him how he could reconcile what he had written in his confessions into a new set of beliefs. They tried to make him feel comfortable and accepted because of his new ideas.

This and other situations prompted Schein's conceptual model for changing attitudes and behavior, which follows a similar three-step process (see Figure 7.3). The model is applicable in a wide range of situations, including the introduction of change to improve motivation in a DP department. The first step of the process is what he calls *unfreezing*. At this step the individual must perceive a need for changing behavior. This need can arise either because individuals feel some aspect of their behavior is inadequate, or because they identify the opportunity for simply improving their behavior.

The second step in Schein's model is the *change* itself. Here the individuals must see the change as their own and incorporate it into their own behavior patterns. This requires that the individual be fully involved in developing the change and in implementing it.

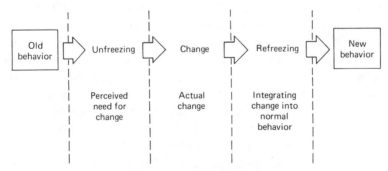

Figure 7.3 Model of Change

The final step of this change process is *refreezing*. The change that has been made in the second step must be personally incorporated into the individual's everday pattern of behavior. Effective refreezing ensures that individuals will not easily go back to the former behavior.

Some examples of how this unfreezing, change, and refreezing have been used will make the relevance of this process much more apparent.[9] The first comes from a course in speed reading called Reading Dynamics. This course advertises that the reader can triple reading speed within a very short period of time. To unfreeze the individual, the Reading Dynamics Institute offers free introductory sessions to potential customers to demonstrate how easy it is to improve reading speed and thus to convince them of the need for making such an improvement. The institute then offers sessions that teach the technique of speed reading. It is in these sessions that individuals make the changes necessary in their own behavior in order to read much faster. Finally, for refreezing, the institute offers "whip" sessions, or refreezing sessions, that are aimed at reinforcing the individuals' use of technique and ensuring that they do not go back to their old reading habits. The last step of refreezing is undoubtedly where Reading Dynamics is weak. This is often the place where learning situations are weak.

In the earlier example of the priest who was being brainwashed, this refreezing step was the downfall of those directing the brainwashing. One day the priest heard children singing outside of his prison window. They were singing a song that he had taught them. Just this one instance was enough to awaken the old attitudes of the priest, and he immediately went back to his old self.

This three-step process of unfreezing, change, and refreezing can be used by any employee (subordinate or manager) who seeks to change his or her own behavior.

Conclusion

The preceding material identifies proper managerial responses once the scope of the task and the employee's
need for growth have been identified. A tool is available to
identify these characteristics as well as to ascertain the
quality of the organization's motivational environment.
Through the use of a diagnostic device such as the JDS/DP
(Job Diagnostic Survey for Data Processing) DP management can compare employee perceptions (in all DP jobs) to
the national norms.

Typically, some jobs need restructuring to improve
their motivating potential. The procedure described in
Chapter 4 and Appendix VI can be utilized for this purpose. Moreover, the same procedure is appropriate for
fine-tuning jobs where the motivational environment is
satisfactory.

In the dynamic DP industry, reassessment of employee
perceptions should be made no less than every two years.
Theoretically, with a 25 percent turnover, we have a new
employee population every four years. Practically, some
areas of the DP division (like the systems department)
have high turnover, whereas others (like the operations
department) are relatively stable. Periodic use of a diagnostic instrument keeps management appraised of the degree of match between each job's motivating potential and
the incumbent's need for growth.

Our industry has placed a lot of emphasis on keeping
pace with the advances in technology. To enable employee
productivity to keep pace with technological improvements—and to be able to keep pace with the demand for
new systems and sytem modifications—equal concern
needs to be placed on the motivational environment.

Because of the increasing demand for services, the DP manager's job will continue to be like the balloon being squeezed from all sides until a weak surface causes a portion (a problem) to pop up, out of proportion to the remaining surface. But, with a sound motivational environment, where employees are satisfied and producing well, the pressures are confined to external sources.

Fortunately, the approach to improving motivation and productivity is equally valuable in increasing job satisfaction. With the improvement in employee satisfaction, the manager's satisfaction level will also be enhanced. Efforts to improve the motivational environment put into play a number of mutually benefical forces.

Notes

1   R. W. Griffin, "Task Design Determinants of Effective Leader Behavior," *Academy of Management Review,* Vol. 4, No. 2, 1979, pp. 215–224.

2   J. R. Hackman and E. E. Lawler, III, "Employee Reactions to Job Characteristics," *Journal of Applied Psychology Monograph,* Vol. 55, 1971, pp. 259–286.

3   R. J. House and G. Dessler, "The Path-Goal Theory of Leadership: Some Post Hoc and A Pnon Tests," in J. G. Hunt and L. L. Larson (eds.), *Contingency Approaches to Leadership* (Carbondale: Southern Illinois University Press, 1974), pp. 29–55.

4   R. J. House and T. R. Mitchell, "Path-Goal Theory of Leadership," *Journal of Contemporary Business,* Vol. 3, Autumn 1974, pp. 31–98.

5   T. Mitchell, "Motivation and Participation: An Integration," *Academy of Management Journal,* Vol. 15, 1973 pp. 160–179.

6   Griffin, "Task Design," p. 220.

7 Ibid.

8 Edgar H. Schein, "Management Development as a Process of Influence," *Industrial Management Review,* Vol. 2, May 1961.

9 S. C. Wheelwright and Spyros Makridakis, *Forecasting Methods for Management* New York: Wiley-Interscience, 1973, pp. 239–241.

OUTPUT FROM COMPUTER PROCESSING OF THE JOB DIAGNOSTIC SURVEY (JDS/DP) LONG FORM

The long form of the JDS/DP measures characteristics of jobs, the reactions of the respondents to their jobs, and the GNS of the respondents.

Each variable measured by the JDS is listed below, along with a brief description of the variable.

I **Job dimensions**   Objective characteristics of the job itself.

   A   *Skill Variety*   The degree to which a job requires a variety of different activities in carrying out the work, which involves the use of a number of different skills and talents of the employee.

   B   *Task Identity*   The degree to which the job requires the completion of a "whole" and identifiable piece of work—that is, doing a job from beginning to end with a visible outcome.

   C   *Task Significance*   The degree to which the job has a substantial impact on the lives or work of other people—whether in the immediate organization or in the external environment.

D *Autonomy* The degree to which the job provides substantial freedom, independence, and
discretion to the employee in scheduling his
work and in determining the procedures to be
used in carrying it out.

E *Feedback from the Job Itself* The degree to
which carrying out the work activities required
by the job results in the employee obtaining
information about the effectiveness of his or her
performance.

F *Feedback from Supervisors* The degree to which
employees receive information about their performance from supervisors. (This construct is
not a job characteristic per se, and is included
only to provide information supplementary to
construct E above).

II **Goal Clarity, Difficulty, Acceptance, Participation,
and Feedback on Goal Accomplishment** These
scales measure the degree to which the employees
understand and accept organizational goals.
Further, it taps into the employees' feelings about
goalsetting participation, goal difficulty, and feedback on goal accomplishment.

III **Skill-Variety, Task Identity, Task Significance, and
Autonomy (Group)** These scales measure four of
the basic job dimensions defined in I above. However, these dimensions refer to the *work group*.

IV **Informal Dimensions**

A **Informal Controls and Pressure** This dimension
indicates the degree of informal control contrasted with formal authority.

B *Skills* This dimension measures employees' desires to learn new skills.

C *Commitment* This dimension measures employees' commitment to the organization and work group.

D *Intragroup Competition* This variable measures the degree of competition within groups contrasted with individuals.

E *Intergroup Competition* This variable measures the degree of competition between groups as contrasted with individuals.

V **Measure of Satisfaction** The private, affective reactions or feelings employees get from working at their jobs.

A *General Satisfaction* An overall measure of the degree to which the employee is satisfied and happy in his or her work.

B *Satisfaction with Co-Workers* The degree to which employees are satisfied and happy with their co-workers.

C *Satisfaction with Supervisors* The degree to which employees are satisfied and happy with their supervisors.

D *Pay Satisfaction* The degree to which employees perceive their pay as equitable.

VI **Need Strength** This is a measure of felt need or desire.

A *Growth Need Strength* This scale taps the degree to which an employee has strong versus weak desire to obtain "growth" satisfaction from his or her work.

B *Social Need Strength* This is a measure of the degree to which the employee wants to interact and socialize with other employees both on and off the job.

C *Need for Achievement* This is a measure of employees' desire to achieve as a person.

D *Existence Need Strength* This scale measures the employees' need for stability and security.

VII Computer Problem Dimensions These four scales measure employees' perceptions of problems associated with computers. The degree of the problem is directly proportional to the rating.

A Maintenance time.

B Access to computer.

C Access to people.

D Realistic schedules.

VIII Individual Recognition These five scales measure employees' perception for the degree of individual recognition they receive for the following:

A Meeting goals.

B Quality.

C Meeting schedules.

D Creativity.

E Motivating co-workers.

IX Compensation Dimensions These nine scales give employees an opportunity to indicate which items are most important to them. They are told to assume an organization pays them one set amount

(100 percent) but allows them to allocate portions of their pay among the following items:

A Base pay percent.
B Hospitalization percent.
C Dental percent.
D Travel percent.
E Tuition percent.
F Professional dues percent.
G Retirement percent.
H Other percent.
I Total percent—should equal 100 percent.

X **Group Motivating Potential** A score reflecting the potential of the group for eliciting positive internal work motivation on the part of the employees.

XI **Motivating Potential Score** A score reflecting the potential of a job for eliciting positive internal work motivation on the part of employees (especially those with high desire for growth need satisfaction)

$$\begin{array}{l} \text{motivating} \\ \text{potential} \\ \text{score (MPS)} \end{array} = \left[\frac{\text{skill variety} + \text{task identity} + \text{task significance}}{3} \right] \times$$

$$\left[\text{autonomy} \right] \times \left[\begin{array}{c} \text{feedback} \\ \text{from the} \\ \text{job} \end{array} \right]$$

XII **Experienced Meaningfulness** This scale is a measure of how worthwhile or important the work is to the employees.

XIII **Experienced Responsibility** This scale measures the employees' beliefs that they are personally accountable for the outcomes of their efforts.

XIV **Knowledge of Results** This scale measures the employees' beliefs that they can determine, on some fairly regular basis, whether the outcomes of their work are satisfactory.

OUTPUT FROM COMPUTER PROCESSING OF THE JOB DIAGNOSTIC SURVEY (JDS) SHORT FORM

The short form of the Job Diagnostic Survey (JDS) measures several characteristics of jobs, the reactions of the respondents to their jobs, and the growth need strength of the respondents.

Each variable measured by the JDS short form is listed below, along with a one- or two-sentence description of the variable.

I **Job Dimensions** Objective characteristics of the job itself.

   A *Skill Variety* The degree to which a job requires a variety of different activities in carrying out the work, which involve the use of a number of different skills and talents of the employee.

   B *Task Identity* The degree to which the job requires the completion of a "whole" and identifiable piece of work—that is, doing a job from beginning to end with a visible outcome.

C *Task Significance* The degree to which the job has a substantial impact on the lives or work of other people—whether in the immediate organization or in the external environment.

D *Autonomy* The degree to which the job provides substantial freedom, independence, and discretion to the employee in scheduling his work and in determining the procedures to be used in carrying it out.

E *Feedback from the Job Itself* The degree to which carrying out the work activities required by the job results in the employee obtaining information about the effectiveness of his or her performance.

F *Feedback from Agents* The degree to which the employee receives information about his or her performance effectiveness from supervisors or from co-workers. (This construct is *not* a job characteristic per se, and is included only to provide information supplementary to construct E above).

II **Measures of Satisfaction** The private, affective reactions or feelings an employee gets from working on his/her job.

A *General Satisfaction* An overall measure of the degree to which the employee is satisfied and happy in his or her work.

B *Internal Work Motivation* The degree to which the employee is *self*-motivated to perform effectively on the job.

C *Specific Satisfactions* These short scales top several specific aspects of the employees' job satisfaction.

C1 *Pay Satisfaction* The degree to which the employee believes his or her pay is equitable.

C2 *Security Satisfaction* The degree to which the employee feels secure in the organization.

C3 *Social Satisfaction* The degree to which the organization meets the needs of the employee to interact with other employees.

C4 *Supervisory Satisfaction* The degree to which employees are satisfied with their supervisors.

C5 *Growth Satisfaction* The degree to which the organization meets the needs of the employees to grow and develop as people.

III Individual Growth Need Strength This scale taps the degree to which an employee has strong vs. weak desire to obtain "growth" satisfactions from his or her work.

IV Motivating Potential Score A score reflecting the potential of a job for eliciting positive internal work motivation on the part of employees (especially those with high desire for growth need satisfaction)

$$
\begin{array}{l}
\text{motivating} \\
\text{potential} \\
\text{score (MPS)}
\end{array}
=
\left[
\frac{\text{skill variety} + \text{task identity} + \text{task significance}}{3}
\right]
\times
\left[\text{autonomy}\right]
\times
\left[\begin{array}{c}\text{feedback} \\ \text{from the} \\ \text{job}\end{array}\right]
$$

V Other Dimensions

A *Job Security*   This measures how the employees feel about retaining their job.

B *Value High Salary and Benefits*   This dimension indicates how the employees value the total compensation package. It is a measure of the priority they assign to compensation.

C *Quick Promotions Value*   This is a measure of the priority employees place on rapid advancement.

D *Social Need Strength*   This dimension is the need that employees have to interact and socialize with other employees both on and off the job.

E *Experienced Meaningfulness*   This scale is a measure of how worthwhile or important the work is to the employees.

F *Experienced Responsibility*   This scale measures the employees' beliefs that they are personally accountable for the outcomes of their efforts.

G *Knowledge of Results*   This scale measures the employees' beliefs that they can determine, on some fairly regular basis, whether the outcomes of their work are satisfactory.

H *Dealing with Others*   The degree to which the job requires the employee to work closely with other people (whether other organization members or organizational "clients").

THE SUPERVISOR
AS COUNSELOR*

As Fred Fiedler has reminded us in a recent *Psychology Today* article (1973), ship captains once could actually whip sailors who didn't obey orders; managers could fire people on the spot for slacking off; students could be expelled from school for talking back to teachers. Today, all that has changed. Sailors are permitted to grow sideburns; unions protect workers from being fired outright for anything other than a major transgression of the rules; students are asked for their suggestions and even for their opinions.

The person in charge used to have unquestioned authority to command and compel. Today, supervisors must focus on persuading rather than ordering workers to perform. They must learn how to convince workers to achieve their objectives or change their behavior.

How can the supervisor do this effectively? One of the best ways is through counseling.

The word *counselor* has been abused lately. Counselors run the gamut from well-trained professionals to amateurs who deal in such unscientific areas as loan

*Reprinted by permission of the publisher from Robert A. Zawacki and Peter E. LaSota, *Supervisory Management,* November 1973. © 1973 by AMACOM, a division of American Management Associations. All rights reserved.

counseling and even funeral counseling. The "true" counselor is a trained expert who understands the application of behavioral science concepts to human relations. Supervisors cannot hope to become "professional" counselors without extensive training and certification, but they can improve their counseling skills to the point where they can use them to effectively persuade subordinates to be more productive.

Role Conflict

Of all the roles that a supervisor may fill in his daily life (father or mother, son or daughter, husband or wife, disciplinarian, leader, etc), the role of counselor may be the most difficult for him to understand. One reason for this is that some supervisors find their role as counselor in conflict with their role as disciplinarian. This is often the result of poor or inadequate management training and a lack of understanding about how to shift from one to another.

Change Your Perceptions

To simplify this problem of role conflict, think of the counseling role in terms of a helper/receiver relationship rather than a counselor/client one. Both helper and receiver must understand that the helper is trying to influence and change the behavior of the receiver in a way that will be useful to both of them.

In the helper/receiver relationship, both parties have needs, values, and feelings that influence their behavior in the relationship. In the old days, the supervisor could tell the receiver what was best for him without any interaction or without considering the subordinate's needs, values, and feelings—unless the supervisor was extraordinarily sensitive. The receiver—either through fear of losing his job or respect for the supervisor or both—often carried out the supervisor's prescriptions. But the supervisor was sharing the responsibility for the outcome of his recommendation. If the receiver carried out the supervisor's recommendation and it failed, the receiver could always blame the supervisor for having given poor advice.

Self-Concept

Before a supervisor can even begin to counsel a subordinate, he should understand what is likely to go on in a particular subordinate's mind while he is being counseled. To get anywhere close to the mark, he must know as much as possible about the subordinate's personality, feelings, and attitudes.

Each of us has created an image of himself—an image variously tagged by behavioral scientists as the "self-image," the "self-structure," or the "self-concept." Regardless of the label used, each of us has a system of ideas and beliefs about himself accumulated through many life experiences.

Here are some important things to remember about a subordinate's self-concept that will directly affect your counseling relationship with him: (1) It is a pattern of beliefs developed over a long period of time; (2) he has a deepseated need to preserve this system of ideas about himself; and (3) in most cases, he will not only want to preserve it, but also to enhance or improve it.

Behavioral researchers have found that people cope with a threat to their self-concept by exhibiting defensive behavior or by changing their self-concept and, possibly, their actions. The greater the threat to the person, the more negative his reaction will be to counseling efforts.

Present Alternatives

If most people react this way when they are threatened, how can you hope to counsel a subordinate without injuring his self-esteem, provoking defensive behavior, or incurring his wrath toward you? One approach proven to be helpful is presenting the subordinate with several alternatives. The process is known as maximizing alternatives.

If both people in the helping relationship agree that there is a problem and that the receiver's behavior is unacceptable, then you have a foundation for beginning to explore alternative kinds of actions you can *both* take.

If the helper can get the receiver to understand and explore the various courses of action available to him, the helper has taken a positive step toward solving the problem or getting the subordinate to modify his behavior.

The key to effective counseling is giving the receiver the freedom to choose the course of action that he feels is best for him under the circumstances. The receiver will be much more likely to carry out a course of action that he himself has identified—because it is his decision and he is responsible for the outcome.

The helper can do his part by using the counseling relationship to let the receiver know exactly what is expected of him. This may include joint goalsetting, better peer relations, increased promptness, greater efficiency in performing his job. If the supervisor has tried to help the receiver explore alternatives and arrive at a personal decision, he can be more certain that his counseling will achieve the desired change.

Counseling Guidelines

If you want to be a more effective counselor, here are some guidelines to help you get the most out of the helper/receiver relationship:

1 *Don't argue* The subordinate will try to preserve his self-concept by meeting your arguments with resistance. If you increase your argumentative position or continue to "pound away" at him, you will achieve even more resistance and denial.

2 *Be prepared to listen* You must understand the subordinate's point of view before you can begin to jointly explore alternatives. Understanding a subordinate's point of view, however, does not mean that you must agree with or support his position. There's a difference between empathy and sympathy.

   Let the subordinate do more than half the talking. It may be easy for you, because of your experience as a supervisor, to get trapped in a prescribing or lecturing role. But a "know-it-all" position may threaten the receiver so much that he mentally leaves the scene or acts more defensively than he would if you were more receptive.

3 *Direct your comments to behavior that the subordinate can change* By giving people unfavorable feedback about

actions over which they have little or no control, you only increase their feelings of frustration and their need to defend themselves.

4 *Give timely feedback* Feedback is most helpful to a subordinate when it is given at the earliest opportunity after an event or interaction has occurred.

Research in this area indicates that people may have a certain tolerance level for accepting unfavorable feedback. When this level is approached or surpassed, no further learning takes place. For this reason, you should give feedback often and in small quantities. Feedback limited to a comprehensive, once-a-year performance review with a subordinate will not help him develop on the job. It may even hinder his growth. Small changes effected over a long period of time will be better for the subordinate and better for you.

5 *Look at subordinates as subjects—not objects that make up your personnel resource* They are human beings with feelings, needs, and values of their own. Try to see the world from their point of view.

6 *Reflect the feelings of the worker* If you can focus on reflecting back the feelings and attitudes of the worker instead of giving advice, the worker will be better able to find his own solution.

When the supervisor bounces back the feelings that the subordinate gives off, the worker can continue to talk about them. Frequent use of "Uhn-huhn," "I see," and "Is that so?" will help bounce the conversational ball back over the net and give the subordinate a chance to elaborate.

7 *Ask skilled questions* The skillful counselor should avoid questions that can be answered with a simple *yes* or *no*. By starting questions with "How do you feel

about . . . ?" or "What do you think about . . . ?" you give the worker a better chance to let his feelings and attitudes emerge along with a multitude of irrelevant facts, details, and excuses. Since the purpose of the session is to solve a problem, past facts are far less important than present feelings and attitudes.

8 *Be on the lookout for signals that the subordinate is willing to commit himself to change or ownership in the outcome of the helper/receiver relationship.* Once a subordinate assumes responsibility for overcoming his or her own shortcomings, your task as a counselor is almost complete.

Reference

Fiedler, F. E. "The trouble with leadership training is that it doesn't train leaders." *Psychology Today,* February 1973, pp. 23–24.

PROCEDURE FOR WORK REDESIGN

The procedure for work redesign is as follows:

1 Begin with a workshop for management, identifying the goals and procedures of the project. Explain the theories of motivation and feedback channels.

2 Conduct workshops for employees and first-line supervisors, by natural work group, discussing work motivation and characteristics of good jobs. Provide employees feedback on the job profile as determined by the JDS/DP.

3 Conduct two-hour brainstorming sessions with all employees to solicit proposals for improving jobs. Divide employees into groups of twelve or fewer. The consultant must create a "psychological contract" with the employees:
   a We sincerely solicit your ideas and suggestions.
   b However, we may or may not implement your ideas (because of organization constraints).
   c Regardless of our decision, we will give you feedback on why or why not your idea was not implemented.

4 Capture all suggestions by using a tape recorder and transcribe to a list distributed to all participants.

5   Use an evaluation committee (comprised of supervisors and nonsupervisors) to screen, consolidate, and determine the feasibility of suggested changes. If a proposal is rejected, record and disseminate the reasons.

6   Get top management's approval of any recommended changes.

7   Prioritize and schedule proposed work changes.

8   Follow-up through formal audits; report results to all employees in a newsletter.

9   Repeat this process periodically (depending on the dynamic characteristics of the organization; typically, once every two years).

NATIONAL NORMS CONCERNING MOTIVATION OF ANALYSTS AND PROGRAMMERS

J. Daniel Couger, Robert A. Zawacki, and Edward B. Oppermann

Working Paper—Information Systems
WP-IS001

Graduate School of Business Administration
University of Colorado
Colorado Springs

December 1979

The Job Diagnostic Survey (JDS/DP) measures several characteristics of jobs, the reactions of the respondents to their jobs, and the GNS of the respondents. The findings in this working paper are based on a sample survey of analysts and programmers.

Each variable measured by the JDS/DP is listed below, along with a one- or two-sentence description of the variable.

1 *Skill Variety* (Skillvar) is a measure of the degree to which a job requires a variety of different activities in carrying out the work, which involve the use of a number of different skills and talents of the employee.

2 *Task Identity* (Taskiden) is a measure of the degree to which the job requires the completion of a "whole and identifiable piece of work"—that is, doing a job from beginning to end with a visible outcome.

3 *Task Significance* (Tasksign) is a measure of the degree to which the job has a substantial impact on the lives or work of other people—whether in the immediate organization or in the external environment.

4 *Experienced Meaningfulness* (Exmeangf) is a measure of how worthwhile or important the work is to the employees.

5 *Autonomy* (Autonomy) is a measure of the degree to which the job provides substantial freedom, independence, and discretion to the employee in scheduling his work and in determining the procedures to be used in carrying it out.

6 *Experienced Responsibility* (Exprespn) is a measure of the employees' beliefs that they are personally accountable for the outcome of their efforts.

7 *General Satisfaction* (Gensatis) is a measure of the degree to which the employee is satisfied and happy with her or his work.

8 *Individual Growth Need Strength* (Ingrnest) is a measure of the degree to which an employee has a strong or weak desire to obtain "growth" satisfactions from his or her work.

9 *Feedback from the Job Itself* (Feedbjob) is a measure of the degree to which carrying out the work activities required by the job results in the employee obtaining

information about the effectiveness of his or her performance.

10 *Feedback from Supervisors* (Feedbsup) is a measure of the degree to which employees receive information about their performance from supervisors.

11 *Knowledge of Results* (Knwldres) is a measure of the employees' beliefs that they can determine on some fairly regular basis whether the outcomes of their work are satisfactory.

12 *Motivating Potential for Individuals* (Motpotin) is a measure of the degree to which the job of individual employee elicits positive work motivation.

13 *Social Need Strength* (Socndstr) is a measure of the degree to which the employee wants to interact and socialize with other employees both on and off the job.

14 *Social Satisfaction* (Socsatis) is a measure of the degree to which employees are satisfied and happy with their co-workers.

15 *Supervisory Satisfaction* (Supsatis) is a measure of the degree to which employees are satisfied and happy with their supervisors.

Table V.1 Internal Consistency Reliabilities of Measurements

Variable Scale	N	Reliability
Skillvar	3	.73
Taskiden	3	.70
Tasksign	3	.73
Exmeangf	9	.71
Autonomy	3	.75
Exprespn	3	.75
Gensatis	2	.59
Ingrnest	6	.76
Feedbjob	4	.76
Feedbsup	3	.87
Knwldres	7	.84
Motpotin	16	.79
Socndstr	3	.60
Socsatis	3	.67
Supsatis	3	.83

N = Number of items composing each scale.

Reliabilities were calculated with the SPSS Scale Reliability Analysis Subprogram for split half coefficients using Spearman-Brown formula.

Table V.2 Means, Standard Deviations, and Intercorrelations

Variable		X̄	S.D.	(1)	(2)	(3)	(4)	(5)	(6)	(7)	(8)	(9)	(10)	(11)	(12)	(13)	(14)	(15)	(16)	(17)	(18)	(19)	(20)
Skillvar	(1)	5.408	1.106	1.00																			
Taskiden	(2)	5.205	1.110	.39	1.00																		
Tasksign	(3)	5.605	1.176	.44	.41	1.00																	
Exmeangf	(4)	5.406	.882	.78	.77	.80	1.00																
Autonomy	(5)	5.290	1.098	.52	.52	.35	.59	1.00															
Exprespn	(6)	5.290	1.098	.52	.52	.35	.59	1.00	1.00														
Gensatis	(7)	5.299	1.163	.35	.26	.28	.38	.40	.40	1.00													
Ingmest	(8)	5.905	.994	.11	.03	.11	.11	.04	.04	.01	1.00												
Feedbjob	(9)	5.133	1.066	.33	.36	.34	.44	.33	.33	.37	.05	1.00											
Feedbsup	(10)	3.966	1.559	.27	.23	.24	.31	.25	.25	.44	.03	.38	1.00										
Knwldres	(11)	4.550	1.097	.35	.33	.33	.43	.34	.34	.49	.05	.75	.89	1.00									
Motpotin	(12)	153.581	62.464	.63	.64	.58	.79	.78	.78	.46	.11	.74	.39	.64	1.00								
Socndstr	(13)	4.200	1.210	.05	-.03	.06	.03	.04	.04	.07	.24	-.01	.09	.06	.02	1.00							
Socsatis	(14)	5.094	1.165	.21	.08	.17	.20	.16	.16	.26	.38	.16	.21	.22	.02	.29	1.00						
Supsatis	(15)	4.910	1.480	.24	.24	.27	.32	.32	.32	.54	.07	.35	.61	.60	.41	.13	.36	1.00					
Sex	(16)	1.262	.450	.04	.02	.01	.03	-.02	-.02	.09	-.02	.03	.12	.10	.02	.08	.02	.09	1.00				
Marital status	(17)	1.626	.487	.06	.08	.17	.14	.05	.05	.06	-.03	-.01	.05	.03	.06	-.01	-.02	.06	-.05	1.00			
Age	(18)	2.939	.913	-.00	.03	.05	.03	.03	.03	.07	-.14	.09	-.07	-.01	.08	-.06	-.00	.05	-.07	.13	1.00		
Education	(19)	4.594	.702	-.01	.01	-.11	-.05	-.01	-.01	-.06	-.07	.00	.01	.00	-.03	-.02	-.16	.03	-.04	-.02	-.09	1.00	
Experience	(20)	2.728	1.419	.11	.10	.15	.16	.07	.07	.07	-.08	.10	-.07	.00	.14	.02	.08	.02	.05	.15	.48	-.26	1.00

(For |r| ≥ .08, p value < .05)

N = 709,
Variables are scored as follows:

(1) through (15) 1,2,3,4,5,6,7.
(16) Male = 1; female = 2.
(17) Single = 1; married = 2.
(18) Under twenty = 1; twenties = 2; thirties = 3; forties = 4; fifties = 5; sixties = 6.
(19) Grade = 1; some high = 2; high = 3; some college = 4; B.A. or B.S. = 5; M.A. or M.S. = 6.
(20) 1 year or less = 1; 1 to 4 years = 2; 4 to 8 years = 3; 8 to 12 years = 4; 12 to 16 years = 5; over 16 years = 6.

153

Table V.3 Variable Means and Standard Deviations by Sex

Variable	Female ($n = 183$)		Male ($n = 526$)		Single-Factor ANOVA	
	$\overline{X}$	SD	$\overline{X}$	SD	F	p value
Skillvar	5.503	1.056	5.377	1.121	1.763	.185
Taskiden	5.260	1.079	5.187	1.120	.588	.444
Tasksign	5.646	1.109	5.595	1.197	.252	.616
Exmeang	5.470	.865	5.387	.886	1.210	.272
Autonom?	5.268	1.066	5.302	1.109	.129	.719
Exprespn	5.268	1.066	5.302	1.109	.129	.719
Gensatis	5.500	1.054	5.233	1.191	7.230*	.007
Ingrnest	5.900	.951	5.909	1.006	.011	.916
Feedbjob	5.206	1.148	5.107	1.036	1.169	.280
Feedbsup	4.282	1.536	3.858	1.554	10.162*	.002
Knwldres	4.744	1.145	4.483	1.073	7.778*	.005
Motpotin	156.914	62.598	152.548	62.323	.665	.415
Socndstr	4.365	1.214	4.139	1.207	4.739*	.030
Socsatis	5.158	1.223	5.069	1.147	.797	.372
Supsatis	5.162	1.419	4.825	1.493	7.097*	.008

*Significant at .05 level.

Table V.4 Variable Means and Standard Deviations by Marital Status

Variable	Married ($n = 442$)		Single ($n = 266$)		Single-Factor ANOVA	
	$\overline{X}$	SD	$\overline{X}$	SD	$\overset{.}{F}$	p value
Skillvar	5.464	1.117	5.319	1.083	2.835	.093
Taskiden	5.280	1.072	5.085	1.162	5.167*	.023
Tasksign	5.772	1.054	5.333	1.309	23.921*	.000
Exmeangf	5.505	.851	5.246	.908	14.668*	.000
Autonomy	5.342	1.035	5.208	1.192	2.492	.115
Exprespn	5.342	1.035	5.208	1.192	2.492	.115
Gensatis	5.335	1.124	5.211	1.220	2.582	.108
Ingrnest	5.887	1.019	5.942	.945	.507	.477
Feedbjob	5.132	1.047	5.137	1.099	.004	.951
Feedbsup	4.023	1.572	3.873	1.537	1.522	.218
Knwldres	4.577	1.110	4.505	1.078	.716	.398
Motpotin	157.030	61.409	148.187	63.792	3.344	.068
Socndstr	4.191	1.193	4.215	1.241	.067	.796
Socsatis	5.077	1.167	5.125	1.162	.286	.593
Supsatis	4.979	1.461	4.798	1.510	2.475	.116

*Significant at .05 level.

Table V.5 Variable Means and Standard Deviations by Age

Variable	20 (N = 257) X̄	SD	30 (N = 297) X̄	SD	40 (N = 104) X̄	SD	50, 60 (N = 52) X̄	SD	Single-Factor ANOVA F	p value
Skillvar	5.363	1.122	5.494	1.047	5.256	1.281	5.436	.949	1.404	.240
Taskiden	5.113	1.062	5.312	1.089	5.115	1.173	5.224	1.291	1.752	.155
Tasksign	5.493	1.260	5.706	1.036	5.565	1.359	5.673	1.069	1.615	.184
Exmeangf	5.323	.881	5.504	.806	5.312	1.054	5.444	.889	2.423	.065
Autonomy	5.239	1.057	5.349	1.074	5.186	1.283	5.429	1.023	1.066	.363
Exprespn	5.239	1.057	5.349	1.074	5.186	1.283	5.429	1.023	1.066	.363
Gensatis	5.313	1.155	5.223	1.184	5.202	1.159	5.870	.923	4.946*	.002
Ingrnest	6.089	.852	5.835	1.054	5.776	1.057	5.635	1.033	5.392*	.001
Feedbjob	5.111	1.092	5.046	1.066	5.202	1.026	5.577	.914	3.898*	.009
Feedbsup	4.256	1.532	3.794	1.544	3.596	1.573	4.282	1.471	7.002*	.000
Knwldres	4.683	1.137	4.420	1.084	4.399	1.034	4.929	.928	5.494*	.001
Motpotin	149.129	61.236	154.500	61.483	151.919	65.559	173.224	65.031	2.209	.086
Socndstr	4.322	1.280	4.167	1.200	3.894	1.092	4.365	1.044	3.509*	.015
Socsatis	5.147	1.119	5.044	1.149	4.971	1.261	5.321	1.287	1.396	.243
Supsatis	5.114	1.425	4.788	1.462	4.612	1.572	5.205	1.513	4.463*	.004

* Significant at .05 level.

Table V.6 Variable Means and Standard Deviations by Education

Variable	High School (N = 31)		Some College (N = 276)		B.A. (N = 350)		M.A. (N = 50)		Single-Factor ANOVA	
	$\overline{X}$	SD	$\overline{X}$	SD	$\overline{X}$	SD	$\overline{X}$	SD	F	p value
Skillvar	5.299	1.330	5.421	1.083	5.435	1.055	5.173	1.405	.932	.425
Taskiden	4.989	1.246	5.208	1.109	5.239	1.105	5.040	1.073	.866	.459
Tasksign	5.531	1.515	5.758	1.130	5.543	1.155	5.220	1.232	3.760*	.011
Exmeangf	5.273	1.190	5.462	.868	5.406	.838	5.144	1.001	2.085	.101
Autonomy	5.344	1.077	5.302	1.173	5.270	1.054	5.307	1.025	.076	.973
Exprespn	5.344	1.077	5.302	1.173	5.270	1.054	5.307	1.025	.076	.973
Gensatis	5.613	1.014	5.305	1.175	5.302	1.118	5.010	1.437	1.790	.148
Ingrnest	5.849	.996	6.005	.943	5.876	1.004	5.583	1.130	2.848*	.037
Feedbjob	5.162	.990	5.101	1.087	5.176	1.036	4.930	1.220	.873	.454
Feedbsup	4.160	1.579	3.881	1.598	4.015	1.531	3.913	1.518	.564	.639
Knwldres	4.661	1.095	4.491	1.128	4.595	1.062	4.422	1.169	.792	.498
Motpotin	154.202	70.156	155.575	62.783	153.077	61.495	142.617	63.521	.612	.608
Socndstr	4.344	1.444	4.195	1.202	4.201	1.201	4.067	1.227	.345	.793
Socsatis	5.430	.804	5.272	1.058	4.981	1.218	4.593	1.341	7.331*	.000
Supsatis	5.161	1.450	4.836	1.503	4.950	1.452	4.807	1.565	.690	.558

*Significant at .05 level.

156

Table V.7 Variable Means and Standard Deviations by Years of Experience

Variable	1 (N = 125) X	SD	1–4 (N = 259) X	SD	4–8 (N = 157) X	SD	8–12 (N = 80) X	SD	12–16 (N = 32) X	SD	>16 (N = 57) X	SD	Single-Factor ANOVA F	p value
Skillvar	5.139	1.135	5.449	1.098	5.408	1.190	5.387	1.133	5.604	.865	5.725	.780	2.731*	.019
Taskiden	4.917	1.046	5.261	1.083	5.234	1.136	5.121	1.218	5.448	1.000	5.480	1.091	2.972*	.012
Tasksign	5.283	1.226	5.554	1.158	5.760	1.140	5.575	1.237	5.906	.992	6.000	1.069	4.336*	.001
Exmeangf	5.113	.837	5.421	.872	5.467	.905	5.361	.929	5.653	.763	5.735	.787	5.204*	.000
Autonomy	5.061	1.267	5.344	.973	5.333	1.189	5.237	1.162	5.344	.796	5.485	.982	1.678	.138
Exprespn	5.061	1.267	5.344	.973	5.333	1.189	5.237	1.162	5.344	.796	5.485	.982	1.678	.138
Gensatis	5.436	1.114	5.160	1.247	5.248	1.136	5.260	1.165	5.453	.928	5.751	.918	3.042*	.010
Ingrnest	6.008	.953	5.914	.992	6.006	.973	5.754	1.130	5.370	.993	5.854	.840	2.896*	.014
Feedbjob	5.036	1.188	5.085	1.088	5.153	1.006	5.009	1.123	5.406	.820	5.504	.781	2.365*	.039
Feedbsup	4.104	1.598	4.094	1.533	3.849	1.663	3.712	1.440	3.531	1.464	4.029	1.441	1.668	.140
Knwldres	4.570	1.187	4.589	1.085	4.501	1.152	4.361	1.066	4.469	.865	4.767	.922	1.094	.362
Motpotin	136.813	61.146	153.677	62.441	157.508	63.046	149.075	67.492	167.282	51.385	177.331	52.290	4.055*	.001
Socndstr	4.347	1.210	4.135	1.259	4.067	1.219	4.275	1.170	4.146	1.244	4.433	.953	1.394	.224
Socsatis	4.880	1.298	5.103	1.105	5.187	1.044	5.021	1.383	4.740	1.223	5.526	.955	3.314*	.006
Supsatis	4.976	1.493	5.010	1.478	4.794	1.560	4.575	1.426	4.635	1.361	5.263	1.274	2.188	.054

*Significant at .05 level.

Table V.8 Summary of Significance Levels—Single-Factor ANOVA

Variable	Sex	Marital Status	Age	Education	Experience
Skillvar	.185	.093	.240	.425	.019*
Taskiden	.444	.023*	.155	.459	.012*
Tasksign	.616	.000*	.184	.011*	.001*
Exmeangf	.272	.000*	.065	.101	.000*
Autonomy	.719	.115	.363	.973	.138
Exprespn	.719	.115	.363	.973	.138
Gensatis	.007*	.108	.002*	.148	.010*
Ingrnest	.916	.477	.001*	.037*	.014*
Feedbjob	.280	.951	.009*	.454	.039*
Feedbsup	.002*	.218	.000*	.639	.140
Knwldres	.005*	.398	.001*	.498	.362
Motpotin	.415	.068	.086	.608	.001*
Socndstr	.030*	.796	.015*	.793	.224
Socsatis	.372	.593	.243	.000*	.006*
Supsatis	.008*	.116	.004*	.558	.054

*p value $< .05$.

NATIONAL NORMS CONCERNING MOTIVATION OF COMPUTER OPERATORS, DATA CONTROL, AND DATA ENTRY PERSONNEL

J. Daniel Couger, Robert A. Zawacki, and Edward B. Oppermann

Working Paper—Information Systems WP-IS-002

Graduate School of Business Administration
University of Colorado
Colorado Springs

December 1979

The Job Diagnostic Survery for Data Processing measures (JDS/DP) general characteristics of jobs, the reactions of the respondents to their jobs, and the GNS of the respondents. The findings in this working paper are based on a sample survey of computer operators, data control, and key entry personnel.

Each variable measured by the JDS is listed below, along with a one- or two-sentence description of the variable.

1 *Skill Variety* (Skillvar) is a measure of the degree to which a job requires a variety of different activities in carrying out the work, which involve the use of a number of different skills and talents of the employee.

2 *Task Identity* (Taskiden) is a measure of the degree to which the job requires the completion of a "whole and identifiable piece of work"—doing a job from beginning to end with a visible outcome.

3 *Task Significance* (Tasksign) is a measure of the degree to which the job has a substantial impact on the lives or work of other people—whether in the immediate organization or in the external environment.

4 *Experienced Meaningfulness* (Exmeangf) is a measure of how worthwhile or important the work is to the employees.

5 *Autonomy* (Autonomy) is a measure of the degree to which the job provides substantial freedom, independence, and discretion to the employee in scheduling work and in determining the procedures to be used in carrying it out.

6 *Experienced Responsibility* (Exprespn) is a measure of the employees' beliefs that they are personally accountable for the outcome of their efforts.

7 *General Satisfaction* (Gensatis) is a measure of the degree to which the employee is satisfied and happy with her or his work.

8 *Individual Growth Need Strength* (Ingrnest) is a measure of the degree to which an employee has a strong or weak desire to obtain "growth" satisfactions from her or his work.

9 *Feedback from the Job Itself* (Feedbjob) is a measure of the degree to which carrying out the work activities required by the job results in the employee obtaining information about the effectiveness of his or her performance.

10 *Feedback from Supervisors* (Feedbsup) is a measure of the degree to which employees receive information about their performance from supervisors.

11 *Knowledge of Results* (Knwldres) is a measure of the employees' beliefs that they can determine on some fairly regular basis whether the outcomes of their work are satisfactory.

12 *Motivating Potential for Individuals* (Motpotin) is a measure of the degree to which the job of individual employee elicits positive work motivation.

13 *Social Need Strength* (Socndstr) is a measure of the degree to which the employee wants to interact and socialize with other employees both on and off the job.

14 *Social Satisfaction* (Socsatis) is a measure of the degree to which employees are satisfied and happy with their co-workers.

15 *Supervisory Satisfaction* (Supsatis) is a measure of the degree to which employees are satisfied and happy with their supervisors.

16 *Dealing with Others* (Dealothr) is a measure of the degree to which the job requires the employee to work closely with other people, whether organizational members or "clients."

17 *Internal Work Motivation* (Intermot) is a measure of the degree to which the employee is self-motivated to perform effectively on the job.

18 *Pay Satisfaction* (Paysatis) is a measure of the degree to which employees perceive their pay as equitable.

19 *Security Satisfaction* (Secsatis) is a measure of the degree to which the employee feels secure in the organization.

20 *Growth Satisfaction* (Grosatis) is a measure of the degree to which the organization meets the needs of the employees to grow and develop as people.

21 *Job Security* (Jobsecur) is a measure of how the employees feel about retaining their job.

22 *Value Salary and Benefits* (Valsalbn) is a dimension that indicates how the employees value the total compensation package. It is a measure of the priority they assign to compensation.

23 *Quick Promotions Value* (Quikprom) is a measure of the priority employees place on rapid advancement.

Table VI.1 Internal Consistency Reliabilities of Measurements

Variable Scale	N	Reliability
Skillvar	3	.63
Taskiden	3	.56
Tasksign	3	.57
Exmeangf	9	.57
Autonomy	3	.66
Exprespn	3	.66
Gensatis	3	.68
Ingrnest	6	.84
Feedbjob	3	.75
Feedbsup	3	.75
Knwldres	6	.82
Motpotin	15	.69
Socsatis	3	.64
Supsatis	4	.67
Dealothr	3	.63
Intermot	4	.68
Paysatis	2	.81
Secsatis	2	.71
Grosatis	4	.83

N = Number of items composing each scale.

Reliabilities were calculated with the SPSS Scale Reliability Analysis subprogram for split-half coefficients using Spearman-Brown formula.

Table VI.2 Means, Standard Deviations, and Intercorrelations

Variable	X̄	S.D.	(1)	(2)	(3)	(4)	(5)	(6)	(7)	(8)	(9)	(10)	(11)	(12)	(13)	(14)	(15)
(1) Skillvar	3.982	1.518	1.00														
(2) Taskiden	4.529	1.393	.16	1.00													
(3) Tasksign	5.615	1.190	.33	.17	1.00												
(4) Exmeangf	4.709	.948	.75	.65	.68	1.00											
(5) Autonomy	4.084	1.540	.49	.26	.22	.48	1.00										
(6) Exprespn	4.084	1.540	.49	.26	.22	.48	1.00	1.00									
(7) Gensatis	4.942	1.347	.32	.17	.21	.34	.32	.32	1.00								
(8) Ingrnest	5.780	1.144	.05	-.02	.18	.09	.04	.04	-.06	1.00							
(9) Feedbjob	4.617	1.445	.38	.20	.26	.41	.41	.41	.33	.07	1.00						
(10) Feedbsup	4.043	1.540	.17	.20	.09	.23	.20	.20	.29	-.04	.38	1.00					
(11) Knwldres	4.330	1.241	.33	.24	.21	.38	.37	.37	.37	.02	.82	.84	1.00				
(12) Motpotin	98.593	65.401	.62	.40	.42	.70	.82	.82	.39	.13	.73	.33	.63	1.00			
(13) Socndstr	5.532	1.656	-.04	-.02	.06	-.01	-.05	-.05	.06	.41	.03	.08	.07	-.00	1.00		
(14) Socsatis	5.067	1.109	.30	.19	.21	.34	.38	.38	.48	.04	.33	.29	.37	.41	.09	1.00	
(15) Supsatis	5.073	1.190	.16	.13	.14	.21	.22	.22	.45	.15	.32	.50	.49	.30	.19	.50	1.00
(16) Dealother	5.032	1.368	.50	.05	.33	.43	.35	.35	.19	.14	.30	.13	.25	.43	.05	.31	.17
(17) Intermot	5.706	1.010	.31	.11	.33	.36	.21	.21	.41	.17	.29	.15	.26	.33	.08	.28	.28
(18) Paysatis	4.231	1.647	.07	.08	.04	.09	.14	.14	.39	-.11	.13	.25	.23	.15	.05	.34	.35
(19) Secsatis	4.865	1.468	.18	.10	.16	.21	.23	.23	.39	.02	.24	.22	.28	.28	.10	.42	.40
(20) Grosatis	4.507	1.366	.50	.25	.29	.51	.54	.54	.67	-.06	.44	.38	.49	.59	.04	.66	.53
(21) Jobsecur	5.869	1.492	.03	.04	.20	.12	.01	.01	.11	.44	.10	.04	.09	.10	.40	.12	.17
(22) Valsalbn	6.227	1.340	.01	.02	.13	.07	-.01	-.01	-.02	.50	.01	-.02	-.01	.04	.36	.05	.12
(23) Quikprom	5.448	1.744	-.02	.03	.10	.04	-.06	-.06	-.04	.53	.00	-.06	-.03	-.00	.29	-.01	.04
(24) Sex	1.719	.455	-.22	.06	-.08	-.12	-.24	-.24	-.06	-.09	-.14	.01	-.08	-.22	.00	-.13	-.03
(25) Marital status	1.614	.487	.10	-.03	.07	.07	.07	.07	.03	.05	.06	-.02	.02	.09	-.01	.04	-.01
(26) Age	3.011	1.132	.18	-.07	.11	.11	.11	.11	.15	-.09	.10	.00	.06	.14	-.09	.11	-.02
(27) Education	3.638	.656	.12	-.02	.04	.08	.05	.05	-.06	.08	.10	.05	.09	.10	-.07	-.05	-.03
(28) Experience	2.975	1.566	.29	-.02	.10	.18	.24	.24	.07	-.04	.14	-.05	.05	.25	-.09	.11	-.06

Table VI.2 (continued)

Variable		$\bar{X}$	SD	(16)	(17)	(18)	(19)	(20)	(21)	(22)	(23)	(24)	(25)	(26)	(27)	(28)
Dealother	(16)	5.032	1.368	1.00												
Intermot	(17)	5.706	1.010	.28	1.00											
Paysatis	(18)	4.231	1.647	.06	.16	1.00										
Secsatis	(19)	4.865	1.468	.20	.22	.43	1.00									
Grosatis	(20)	4.507	1.366	.33	.37	.47	.51	1.00								
Jobsecur	(21)	5.869	1.492	.09	.17	-.00	.06	.08	1.00							
Valsalbn	(22)	6.227	1.340	.08	.07	-.11	.03	-.02	.41	1.00						
Quikprom	(23)	5.448	1.744	.04	.04	-.19	-.00	-.08	.34	.49	1.00					
Sex	(24)	1.719	.455	-.19	-.00	-.01	-.14	-.14	.05	-.01	.04	1.00				
Marital Status	(25)	1.614	.487	.11	.06	.01	.01	.05	.03	.02	-.04	-.05	1.00			
Age	(26)	3.011	1.132	.16	.10	.10	.09	.15	-.01	-.10	-.13	.01	.24	1.00		
Educ	(27)	3.638	.656	.11	-.04	-.03	-.03	-.02	-.06	.05	.01	-.22	-.01	-.08	1.00	
Exper	(28)	2.975	1.566	.27	.07	-.01	.14	.16	.00	-.07	-.09	-.09	.21	.59	-.10	1.00

(For $|r| \geq .06$, p value $< .05$)

$N = 1227$.

Variables are scored as follows:
(1) through (23) 1, 2, 3, 4, 5, 6, 7.
(24) Male = 1; female = 2.
(25) Single = 1; married = 2.
(26) Under twenty = 1; twenties = 2; thirties = 3; forties = 4; fifties = 5; sixties = 6.
(27) Grade = 1; some high = 2; high = 3; some college = 4; B.A. or B.S. = 5; M.A. or M.S. = 6.
(28) 1 year or less = 1; 1 to 4 years = 2; 4 to 8 years = 3; 8 to 12 years = 4; 12 to 16 years = 5; over 16 years = 6.

165

Table VI.3 Variable Means and Standard Deviations by Sex

Variable	Female (N = 884)		Male (N = 347)		Single-Factor ANOVA	
	$\overline{X}$	SD	$\overline{X}$	SD	F	p value
Skillvar	3.769	1.495	4.513	1.448	62.731*	.000
Taskiden	4.576	1.381	4.408	1.405	3.643	.057
Tasksign	5.551	1.223	5.774	1.085	8.816*	.003
Exmeangf	4.632	.934	4.898	.952	20.006*	.000
Autonomy	3.859	1.559	4.662	1.333	71.657*	.000
Exprespn	3.859	1.559	4.662	1.333	71.657*	.000
Gensatis	4.889	1.406	5.065	1.176	4.236*	.040
Ingrnest	5.714	1.204	5.952	.957	10.878*	.001
Feedbjob	4.477	1.486	4.962	1.282	28.502*	.000
Feedbsup	4.038	1.560	4.037	1.487	.000	.986
Knwldres	4.258	1.275	4.499	1.138	9.465*	.002
Motpotin	89.285	63.027	122.236	65.565	66.572*	.000
Socndstr	5.518	1.738	5.536	1.469	.029	.865
Socsatis	4.969	1.169	5.294	.910	21.654*	.000
Supsatis	5.055	1.213	5.118	1.122	.708	.400
Dealothr	4.871	1.374	5.447	1.269	45.738*	.000
Intermot	5.707	1.029	5.702	.962	.006	.939
Paysatis	4.219	1.672	4.248	1.584	.080	.778
Secsatis	4.726	1.540	5.197	1.224	25.973*	.000
Grosatis	4.383	1.419	4.808	1.175	24.479*	.000
Jobsecur	5.909	1.512	5.766	1.435	2.275	.132
Valsolbn	6.217	1.399	6.243	1.202	.091	.763
Quikprom	5.489	1.791	5.336	1.612	1.927	.165

*Significant at .05 level.

Table VI.4   Variable Means and Standard Deviations
by Marital Status

Variable	Married (N = 757)		Single (N = 474)		Single-Factor ANOVA	
	X̄	SD	X̄	SD	F	p value
Skillvar	4.105	1.522	3.784	1.488	13.203*	.000
Taskiden	4.498	1.386	4.584	1.400	1.105	.294
Tasksign	5.679	1.177	5.511	1.205	5.850*	.016
Exmeangf	4.761	.941	4.626	.950	5.916*	.015
Autonomy	4.174	1.590	3.942	1.452	6.614*	.010
Exprespn	4.174	1.590	3.942	1.452	6.614*	.010
Gensatis	4.972	1.351	4.890	1.337	1.078	.299
Ingrnest	5.823	1.099	5.709	1.211	2.902	.089
Feedbjob	4.677	1.438	4.514	1.467	3.662	.056
Feedbsup	4.016	1.548	4.072	1.534	.388	.533
Knwldres	4.346	1.251	4.293	1.240	.528	.468
Motpotin	103.356	68.118	90.953	60.199	10.553*	.001
Socndstr	5.506	1.662	5.549	1.675	.190	.663
Socsatis	5.094	1.126	5.009	1.092	1.679	.195
Supsatis	5.057	1.193	5.093	1.185	.262	.609
Dealothr	5.146	1.381	4.849	1.331	13.910*	.000
Intermot	5.753	.997	5.627	1.026	4.540*	.033
Paysatis	4.238	1.670	4.210	1.611	.084	.772
Secsatis	4.865	1.500	4.852	1.423	.024	.876
Grosatis	4.550	1.346	4.425	1.401	2.439	.119
Jobsecur	4.903	1.484	5.814	1.504	1.032	.310
Valsolbn	6.238	1.317	6.201	1.392	.210	.647
Quikprom	5.398	1.767	5.527	1.700	1.600	.206

*Significant at .05 level.

Table VI.5 Variable Means and Standard Deviations by Age

Variable	20 (N = 37) X	SD	20 (N = 469) X	SD	30 (N = 360) X	SD	40 (N = 206) X	SD	50, 60 (N = 161) X	SD	Single-Factor ANOVA F	p value
Skillvar	3.000	1.281	3.654	1.470	4.165	1.488	4.385	1.540	4.205	1.470	15.910*	.000
Taskiden	4,694	1.292	4.638	1.423	4.453	1.378	4.603	1.398	4.261	1.301	2.780*	.026
Tasksign	5.297	1.071	5.452	1.279	5.691	1.115	5.771	1.147	5.778	1.094	4.931*	.001
Exmeangf	4.330	.806	4.581	.962	4.770	.916	4.920	.981	4.748	.883	6.727*	.000
Autonomy	3.476	1.291	3.899	1.482	4.186	1.521	4.324	1.607	4.226	1.633	5.183*	.000
Exprespn	3.476	1.291	3.899	1.482	4.186	1.521	4.324	1.607	4.226	1.633	5.183*	.000
Gensatis	5.033	1.314	4.759	1.373	4.815	1.363	5.280	1.165	5.275	1.339	8.897*	.000
Ingrnest	5.671	1.161	5.852	1.091	5.873	1.100	5.706	1.201	5.487	1.263	4.053*	.003
Feedbjob	3.928	1.366	4.520	1.440	4.621	1.426	4.766	1.472	4.814	1.462	3.940*	.004
Feedbsup	3.875	1.281	4.058	1.530	4.009	1.540	4.013	1.618	4.096	1.552	.222	.926
Knowldres	3.902	1.153	4.289	1.230	4.315	1.243	4.390	1.292	4.455	1.243	1.756	.136
Motpotin	61.455	33.429	89.165	58.998	102.053	64.020	113.383	77.057	106.778	68.597	9.182*	.000
Socndstr	5.946	1.825	5.682	1.582	5.467	1.677	5.398	1.669	5.280	1.740	2.963*	.019
Socsatis	5.152	1.140	4.915	1.140	5.061	1.021	5.198	1.160	5.284	1.120	4.524*	.001
Supsatis	5.318	1.262	5.096	1.151	5.025	1.146	5.021	1.278	5.106	1.260	.713	.583
Dealothr	4.253	1.093	4.768	1.354	5.211	1.295	5.309	1.421	5.209	1.381	12.104*	.000
Intermot	5.764	.915	5.577	1.062	5.698	.944	5.891	.962	5.834	1.037	4.375*	.002
Paysatis	4.689	1.426	4.028	1.631	4.144	1.578	4.444	1.661	4.587	1.788	5.560*	.000
Secsatis	4.581	1.758	4.719	1.503	4.887	1.362	4.964	1.520	5.100	1.469	2.771*	.026
Grosatis	4.482	1.493	4.269	1.391	4.494	1.297	4.786	1.274	4.825	1.424	8.040*	.000
Jobsecur	5.757	1.623	5.931	1.447	5.818	1.538	5.801	1.512	5.923	1.460	.521	.720
Valsolbn	6.189	1.351	6.369	1.282	6.257	1.297	6.085	1.407	5.925	1.492	4.009*	.003
Quikprom	5.757	1.342	5.667	1.656	5.436	1.749	5.284	1.755	4.977	1.932	5.624*	.000

*Significant at .05 level.

Table VI.6 Variable Means and Standard Deviations by Education

Variable	Some High School (N = 40) X̄	SD	High School (N = 440) X̄	SD	Some College (N = 675) X̄	SD	B.A., M.A. (N = 77) X̄	SD	Single-Factor ANOVA F	p value
Skillvar	3.700	1.322	3.802	1.477	4.037	1.521	4.623	1.616	7.514*	.000
Taskiden	4.733	1.310	4.543	1.325	4.517	1.412	4.511	1.606	.322	.809
Tasksign	5.735	1.359	5.509	1.217	5.661	1.162	5.733	1.155	1.887	.130
Exmeangf	4.723	.958	4.618	.902	4.738	.964	4.956	.992	3.327*	.019
Autonomy	4.067	1.605	4.033	1.525	4.073	1.530	4.510	1.629	2.153	.092
Exprespn	4.067	1.605	4.033	1.525	4.073	1.530	4.510	1.629	2.153	.092
Gensatis	5.083	1.404	5.039	1.271	4.859	1.385	4.951	1.395	1.763	.153
Ingrnest	5.592	1.027	5.694	1.205	5.824	1.107	6.000	1.104	2.481	.060
Feedbjob	4.392	1.414	4.478	1.459	4.653	1.428	5.128	1.492	5.041*	.002
Feedbsup	3.542	1.786	4.047	1.544	4.019	1.531	4.377	1.451	2.670*	.046
Knwldres	3.967	1.371	4.263	1.234	4.336	1.230	4.752	1.302	4.548*	.004
Motpotin	88.774	63.010	93.517	63.267	99.080	64.699	127.702	77.200	6.361*	.000
Socndstr	5.800	1.418	5.627	1.658	5.477	1.677	5.195	1.670	2.120	.096
Socsatis	5.292	1.138	5.080	1.157	5.044	1.091	4.948	1.050	.929	.426
Supsatis	5.165	1.207	5.107	1.191	5.034	1.195	5.127	1.117	.498	.684
Dealothr	4.708	1.270	4.881	1.387	5.109	1.342	5.385	1.448	4.983*	.002
Intermot	5.800	.903	5.725	1.011	5.697	1.006	5.591	1.104	.512	.674
Paysatis	4.591	1.658	4.201	1.695	4.238	1.612	4.045	1.669	1.009	.388
Secsatis	5.063	1.460	4.886	1.495	4.813	1.455	4.909	1.541	.545	.652
Grosatis	4.629	1.272	4.528	1.326	4.455	1.401	4.646	1.360	.718	.542
Jobsecur	6.225	1.050	5.926	1.460	5.847	1.533	5.584	1.445	1.967	.117
Valsalbn	5.950	1.616	6.192	1.404	6.260	1.278	6.315	1.300	.922	.429
Quikprom	5.050	1.894	5.449	1.748	5.473	1.739	5.390	1.671	.770	.511

*Significant at .05 level.

169

Table VI.7 Variable Means and Standard Deviations by Years of Experience

Variable	1 (N = 217)		1–4 (N = 357)		4–8 (N = 263)		8–12 (N = 181)		12–16 (N = 65)		>16 (N = 146)		Single-Factor ANOVA	
	X̄	SD	X̄	SD	X̄	SD	X̄	SD	X̄	SD	X̄	SD	F	p value
Skillvar	3.345	1.382	3.751	1.525	4.045	1.467	4.167	1.447	4.795	1.397	4.768	1.393	23.382*	.000
Taskiden	4.683	1.340	4.533	1.437	4.493	1.419	4.359	1.388	4.437	1.422	4.602	1.278	1.247	.285
Tasksign	5.317	1.273	5.600	1.187	5.679	1.233	5.708	1.073	5.928	1.050	5.715	1.119	4.261*	.001
Exmeangf	4.449	.943	4.628	.937	4.739	.950	4.745	.874	5.053	.901	5.028	.954	9.238*	.000
Autonomy	3.687	1.407	3.821	1.533	4.052	1.558	4.277	1.552	5.118	1.420	4.680	1.340	16.830*	.000
Exprespn	3.687	1.407	3.821	1.533	4.052	1.558	4.277	1.552	5.118	1.420	4.680	1.340	16.830*	.000
Gensatis	5.110	1.349	4.724	1.420	4.873	1.273	4.876	1.267	5.010	1.449	5.389	1.218	6.137*	.000
Ingmest	5.674	1.228	5.921	1.061	5.787	1.183	5.805	1.015	5.921	.983	5.491	1.288	3.576*	.003
Feedbjob	4.429	1.514	4.435	1.493	4.638	1.412	4.676	1.322	4.805	1.540	5.133	1.251	5.993*	.000
Feedbsup	4.476	1.442	3.870	1.525	3.999	1.570	3.888	1.530	4.000	1.549	4.069	1.564	4.846*	.000
Knwldres	4.453	1.259	4.152	1.279	4.319	1.249	4.282	1.195	4.403	1.164	4.601	1.157	3.400*	.005
Motpotin	79.189	53.480	88.241	62.609	98.160	64.648	103.768	63.521	135.219	75.684	130.217	68.942	17.909*	.000
Socndstr	5.664	1.684	5.728	1.594	5.468	1.634	5.320	1.666	5.400	1.739	5.295	1.694	2.653*	.022
Socsatis	5.075	1.179	4.928	1.108	4.945	1.104	5.103	1.022	5.366	1.066	5.413	1.065	5.664*	.000
Supsatis	5.319	1.156	5.077	1.187	4.921	1.160	4.916	1.192	5.335	1.187	5.035	1.240	4.050*	.001
Dealothr	4.466	1.315	4.791	1.389	5.156	1.348	5.297	1.223	5.764	1.244	5.597	1.179	21.888*	.000
Intermot	5.596	1.055	5.692	1.001	5.704	1.004	5.678	.948	5.812	1.024	5.887	1.031	1.639	.147
Paysatis	4.570	1.500	4.091	1.588	3.995	1.669	4.224	1.758	4.431	1.620	4.401	1.733	4.000*	.001
Secsatis	4.482	1.626	4.768	1.521	4.976	1.342	4.945	1.408	4.992	1.388	5.283	1.299	6.254*	.000
Grosatis	4.451	1.402	4.282	1.436	4.379	1.309	4.509	1.351	5.050	1.068	5.102	1.150	10.442*	.000
Jobsecur	5.916	1.510	5.893	1.501	5.760	1.490	5.822	1.532	6.138	1.261	5.876	1.490	.804	.547
Valsalbn	6.218	1.392	6.383	1.220	6.238	1.315	6.146	1.342	6.277	1.269	5.925	1.550	2.630*	.023
Quikprom	5.504	1.664	5.678	1.640	5.478	1.708	5.190	1.897	5.231	1.886	5.144	1.838	3.208*	.007

*Significant at .05 level.

170

Table VI.8 Summary of Significance Levels—Single-Factor ANOVA

Variable	Sex	Marital Status	Age	Education	Experience
Skillvar	.000*	.000*	.000*	.000*	.000*
Taskiden	.057	.294	.026*	.809	.285
Tasksign	.000*	.016*	.001*	.130	.001*
Exmeanfg	.000*	.015*	.000*	.019*	.000*
Autonomy	.000*	.010*	.000*	.092	.000*
Exprespn	.000*	.010*	.000*	.092	.000*
Gensatis	.040*	.299	.000*	.153	.000*
Ingrnest	.001*	.089	.003*	.060	.003*
Feedbjob	.000*	.056	.004*	.002*	.000*
Feedbsup	.986	.533	.926	.046*	.000*
Knwldres	.002*	.468	.136	.004*	.005*
Motpotin	.000*	.001*	.000*	.000*	.000*
Socndstr	.865	.663*	.019*	.096	.022*
Socsatis	.000*	.195	.001*	.426	.000*
Supsatis	.400	.609	.583	.684	.001*
Dealothr	.000*	.000*	.000*	.002*	.000*
Intermot	.939	.033*	.002*	.674	.147
Paysatis	.778	.772	.000*	.388	.001*
Secsatis	.000*	.876	.026*	.652	.000*
Grosatis	.000*	.119	.000*	.542	.000*
Jobsecur	.132	.310	.720	.117	.547
Valsolbn	.763	.647	.003*	.429	.023*
Quikprom	.165	.206	.000*	.511	.007*

*p value $< .05$.

NATIONAL NORMS CONCERNING MOTIVATION OF DP MANAGERS

J. Daniel Couger, Robert A. Zawacki, and Edward B. Opperman

Working Paper—Information Systems
WP-IS003

Graduate School of Business Administration
University of Colorado
Colorado Springs

December, 1979

The Job Diagnostic Survey for Data Processing (JDS/DP) measures several characteristics of jobs, the reactions of the respondents to their jobs, and the GNS of the respondents. The findings in this working paper are based on a sample survey of DP managers.

Each variable measured by the JDS is listed below, along with a one or two sentence description of the variable.

1 *Skill Variety* (Skillvar) is a measure of the degree to which a job requires a variety of different activities in carrying out the work, which involve the use of a number of different skills and talents of the employee.

2 *Task Identity* (Taskiden) is a measure of the degree to which the job requires the completion of a "whole and identifiable piece of work"—that is, doing a job from beginning to end with a visible outcome.

3 *Task Significance* (Tasksign) is a measure of the degree to which the job has a substantial impact on the lives or work of other people—whether in the immediate organization or in the external environment.

4 *Experienced Meaningfulness* (Exmeangf) is a measure of how worthwhile or important the work is to the employees.

5 *Autonomy* (Autonomy) is a measure of the degree to which the job provides substantial freedom, independence, and discretion to the employee in scheduling work and in determining the procedures to be used in carrying it out.

6 *Experienced Responsibility* (Exprespn) is a measure of the employees' beliefs that they are personally accountable for the outcome of their efforts.

7 *General Satisfaction* (Gensatis) is a measure of the degree to which the employee is satisfied and happy with her or his work.

8 *Individual Growth Need Strength* (Ingrnest) is a measure of the degree to which an employee has a strong vs. weak desire to obtain "growth" satisfactions from her or his work.

9 *Feedback from the Job Itself* (Feedbjob) is a measure of the degree to which carrying out the work activities required by the job results in the employee obtaining

information about the effectiveness of his or her performance.

10 *Feedback from Supervisors*   (Feedbsup) is a measure of the degree to which employees receive information about their performance from supervisors.

11 *Knowledge of Results*   (Knwldres) is a measure of the employees' beliefs that they can determine on some fairly regular basis whether the outcomes of their work are satisfactory.

12 *Motivating Potential for Individuals*   (Motpotin) is a measure of the degree to which the job of individual employee elicits positive work motivation.

13 *Social Need Strength*   (Socndstr) is a measure of the degree to which the employee wants to interact and socialize with other employees both on and off the job.

14 *Social Satisfaction*   (Socsatis) is a measure of the degree to which employees are satisfied and happy with their co-workers.

15 *Supervisory Satisfaction*   (Supsatis) is a measure of the degree to which employees are satisfied and happy with their supervisors.

Table VII.1 Internal Consistency Reliabilities of Measurements

Variable Scale	N	Reliability
Skillvar	3	.63
Taskiden	3	.61
Tasksign	3	.64
Exmeangf	9	.63
Autonomy	3	.73
Exprespn	3	.73
Gensatis	2	.53
Ingrnest	6	.86
Feedbjob	4	.64
Feedbsup	3	.80
Knwldres	7	.78
Motpotin	16	.75
Socndstr	3	.59
Socsatis	3	.68
Supsatis	3	.90

N = Number of items composing each scale.

Reliabilities were calculated with the SPSS Scale Reliability Analysis subprogram for split-half coefficients using Spearman-Brown formula.

able VII.2 Means, Standard Deviations, and Intercorrelations

ariable		$\bar{X}$	SD	(1)	(2)	(3)	(4)	(5)	(6)	(7)	(8)
killvar	(1)	6.155	.778	1.00							
askiden	(2)	5.797	.962	.29	1.00						
asksign	(3)	6.307	.748	.38	.23	1.00					
xmeangf	(4)	6.086	.603	.74	.75	.70	1.00				
utonomy	(5)	6.096	.863	.37	.43	.28	.50	1.00			
xprespn	(6)	6.096	.863	.37	.43	.28	.50	1.00	1.00		
ensatis	(7)	5.531	.892	.21	.24	.23	.31	.28	.28	1.00	
ngrnest	(8)	6.322	.689	.28	.21	.20	.31	.22	.22	.13	1.00
eedbjob	(9)	5.246	.938	.27	.36	.35	.45	.34	.34	.27	.19
eedbsup	(10)	4.097	1.454	.22	.21	.18	.28	.18	.18	.32	.10
nwldres	(11)	4.671	.976	.29	.32	.30	.42	.30	.30	.37	.17
lotpotin	(12)	199.086	61.292	.50	.50	.50	.73	.73	.73	.38	.30
ocndstr	(13)	4.511	.994	.05	−.04	.12	.05	.01	.01	.14	.23
ocsatis	(14)	5.848	.731	.31	.24	.26	.37	.30	.30	.47	.27
upsatis	(15)	4.937	1.433	.24	.24	.15	.29	.32	.32	.56	.10
ex	(16)	1.071	.258	−.03	−.02	.06	.00	−.02	−.02	−.00	.09
Marital status	(17)	1.873	.333	.10	−.07	−.02	−.01	−.01	−.01	−.06	−.09
ge	(18)	3.710	.817	.09	.05	.12	.11	.04	.04	−.10	−.04
ducation	(19)	4.968	.836	.20	.05	−.11	.06	.09	.09	−.07	.11
xperience	(20)	3.621	1.502	−.06	−.11	.05	−.06	−.05	−.05	.08	−.06

(For $|r| \geq .09$, p value $< .05$)

$N = 504$.

ariables are scored as follows:

(1) through (15) 1, 2, 3, 4, 5, 6, 7.

(16) Male = 1; female = 2.

(17) Single = 1; married = 2.

(18) Under twenty = 1; twenties = 2; thirties = 3; forties = 4; fifties = 5; sixties = 6.

(19) Grade = 1; some high = 2; high = 3; some college = 4; B.A. or B.S. = 5; M.A. or M.S. = 6.

(20) 1 year or less = 1; 1 to 4 years = 2; 4 to 8 years = 3; 8 to 12 years = 4; 12 to 16 years = 5; over 16 years = 6.

Table VII.2 (continued)

Variable		(9)	(10)	(11)	(12)	(13)	(14)	(15)	(16)	(17)	(18)	(19)
Feedbjob	(9)	1.00										
Feedbsup	(10)	.30	1.00									
Knwldres	(11)	.70	.89	1.00								
Motpotin	(12)	.83	.35	.66	1.00							
Socndstr	(13)	.11	.12	.14	.08	1.00						
Socsatis	(14)	.34	.32	.40	.44	.22	1.00					
Supsatis	(15)	.29	.52	.52	.40	.13	.44	1.00				
Sex	(16)	.00	−.03	−.02	.01	−.18	−.06	−.00	1.00			
Marital status	(17)	−.06	.08	.03	−.04	.02	−.04	.01	−.26	1.00		
Age	(18)	.11	.07	.11	.12	−.02	.15	.04	−.14	.14	1.00	
Education	(19)	−.05	.05	.02	.03	−.00	.04	−.04	−.04	.02	.07	1.00
Experience	(20)	.09	.02	.05	−.00	.01	.07	.02	−.05	.09	.39	−.18

Table VII.3 Variable Means and Standard Deviations by Sex

| Variable | Female (N = 36) | | Male (N = 470) | | Single-Factor ANOVA | |
	$\bar{X}$	SD	$\bar{X}$	SD	F	p value
Skillvar	6.066	.952	6.156	.758	.453	.501
Taskiden	5.722	1.228	5.802	.944	.226	.635
Tasksign	6.472	.525	6.284	.777	2.034	.154
Exmeangf	6.087	.725	6.081	.601	.003	.953
Autonomy	6.037	1.162	6.097	.846	.158	.691
Exprespn	6.037	1.162	6.097	.846	.158	.691
Gensatis	5.530	.736	5.533	.903	.000	.982
Ingrnest	6.556	.565	6.304	.694	4.480*	.035
Feedbjob	5.250	1.042	5.243	.932	.002	.966
Feedbsup	3.935	1.429	4.111	1.454	.487	.485
Knwldres	4.593	.973	4.677	.975	.249	.618
Motpotin	201.625	71.684	198.624	60.782	.079	.778
Socndstr	3.873	1.024	4.560	.973	16.514*	.000
Socsatis	5.699	.934	5.860	.712	1.619	.204
Supsatis	4.918	1.379	4.942	1.438	.009	.924

*Significant at .05 level.

Table VII.4 Variable Means and Standard Deviations by Marital Status

| Variable | Married (N = 442) | | Single (N = 64) | | Single-Factor ANOVA | |
	$\bar{X}$	SD	$\bar{X}$	SD	F	p value
Skillvar	6.176	.757	5.964	.885	4.262*	.040
Taskiden	5.771	.965	5.969	.955	2.354	.126
Tasksign	6.290	.759	6.354	.794	.401	.527
Exmeangf	6.079	.606	6.095	.644	.041	.839
Autonomy	6.089	.907	6.120	.888	.070	.791
Exprespn	6.089	.870	6.120	.888	.070	.791
Gensatis	5.511	.915	5.681	.698	2.021	.156
Ingrnest	6.300	.686	6.479	.688	3.825	.051
Feedbjob	5.223	.953	5.387	.827	1.717	.191
Feedbsup	4.140	1.442	3.807	1.495	2.951	.086
Knwldres	4.682	.988	4.597	.875	.417	.519
Motpotin	197.909	61.838	205.247	59.555	.794	.373
Socndstr	4.520	.983	4.448	1.054	.294	.588
Socsatis	5.838	.726	5.922	.759	.747	.388
Supsatis	4.946	1.440	4.899	1.391	.060	.807

*Significant at .05 level.

Table VII.5 Variable Means and Standard Deviations by Age

Variable	20 (N = 20)		30 (N = 199)		40 (N = 196)		50, 60 (N = 91)		Single-Factor ANOVA	
	$\bar{X}$	SD	$\bar{X}$	SD	$\bar{X}$	SD	$\bar{X}$	SD	F	p value
Skillvar	5.885	.781	6.104	.777	6.192	.787	6.214	.721	1.428	.234
Taskiden	6.050	1.115	5.752	.898	5.739	1.040	5.959	.891	1.699	.166
Tasksign	6.167	.729	6.209	.790	6.352	.742	6.403	.739	2.003	.113
Exmeangf	6.034	.558	6.022	.598	6.094	.635	6.192	.585	1.706	.165
Autonomy	6.133	.847	6.063	.931	6.088	.862	6.159	.851	.267	.849
Exprespn	6.133	.847	6.063	.931	6.088	.862	6.159	.851	.267	.849
Gensatis	5.552	.724	5.448	.951	5.529	.859	5.722	.840	1.988	.115
Ingrnest	6.658	.380	6.317	.673	6.291	.723	6.326	.688	1.734	.159
Feedbjob	5.313	.712	5.134	.938	5.252	.947	5.450	.945	2.422	.065
Feedbsup	4.117	1.534	4.026	1.434	4.028	1.396	4.403	1.569	1.668	.173
Knwldres	4.715	.847	4.580	.958	4.640	.960	4.927	1.034	2.777*	.041
Motpotin	200.834	55.979	191.777	59.768	199.059	61.551	213.360	64.811	2.594	.052
Socndstr	4.350	1.391	4.565	.970	4.488	.986	4.476	.958	.445	.721
Socsatis	5.692	.849	5.745	.783	5.884	.689	6.034	.627	3.824*	.010
Supsatis	4.980	1.295	4.932	1.445	4.829	1.470	5.190	1.341	1.330	.264

*Significant at .05 level.

180

Table VII.6 Variable Means and Standard Deviations by Education

Variable	High School (N = 12) X̄	SD	Some College (N = 149) X̄	SD	B.A. (N = 188) X̄	SD	M.A. (N = 156) X̄	SD	Single-Factor ANOVA F	p value
Skillvar	5.722	1.324	5.982	.801	6.160	.761	6.339	.646	6.961*	.000
Taskiden	5.139	1.446	5.823	.947	5.762	1.016	5.854	.858	2.170	.091
Tasksign	6.389	.763	6.398	.732	6.298	.730	6.203	.818	1.738	.158
Exmeangf	5.750	1.002	6.068	.613	6.073	.611	6.132	.566	1.575	.195
Autonomy	5.778	1.466	6.028	.830	6.067	.934	6.203	.762	1.692	.168
Exprespn	5.778	1.466	6.028	.830	6.067	.934	6.203	.762	1.692	.168
Gensatis	5.419	.764	5.632	.822	5.541	.912	5.431	.934	1.364	.253
Ingrmest	6.056	.871	6.272	.723	6.287	.704	6.435	.609	2.442	.064
Feedbjob	4.750	.989	5.389	.782	5.193	1.040	5.201	.931	2.613	.051
Feedbsup	3.694	1.560	4.051	1.456	4.082	1.491	4.193	1.400	.590	.622
Knwldres	4.222	1.145	4.720	.901	4.637	1.033	4.697	.956	1.086	.354
Motpotin	170.855	76.967	200.631	56.701	196.687	66.783	201.709	58.209	1.057	.367
Socndstr	3.833	.937	4.619	.975	4.468	.984	4.510	1.009	2.593	.052
Socsatis	5.598	1.175	5.873	.698	5.789	.743	5.916	.702	1.396	.243
Supsatis	5.051	1.053	5.015	1.369	4.928	1.452	.876	1.504	.265	.851

*Significant at .05 level.

Table VII.7 Variable Means and Standard Deviations by Experience

Variable	1 (N = 26)		1–4 (N = 119)		4–8 (N = 107)		8–12 (N = 105)		12–16 (N = 66)		16 (N = 82)		Single-Factor ANOVA	
	X̄	SD	X̄	SD	X̄	SD	X̄	SD	X̄	SD	X̄	SD	F	p value
Skillvar	6.038	.949	6.235	.767	6.150	.727	6.227	.694	6.025	.854	6.077	.788	1.102	.358
Taskiden	5.936	.914	5.892	1.036	5.876	.910	5.808	.844	5.715	1.029	5.580	1.010	1.425	.214
Tasksign	6.115	.957	6.283	.791	6.255	.808	6.406	.592	6.278	.834	5.350	.635	.904	.478
Exmeangf	6.030	.782	6.137	.613	6.094	.570	6.147	.523	6.006	.675	6.002	.600	.981	.429
Autonomy	6.050	.861	6.176	.982	6.097	.842	6.160	.818	5.994	.796	6.008	.825	.683	.636
Exprespn	6.050	.861	6.176	.982	6.097	.842	6.160	.818	5.994	.796	6.008	.825	.683	.636
Gensatis	5.523	.656	5.460	.922	5.497	.870	5.516	.972	5.544	.914	5.702	.820	.792	.555
Ingrnest	6.481	.604	6.379	.647	6.292	.718	6.297	.742	6.280	.732	6.289	.633	.595	.704
Feedbjob	4.981	1.005	5.162	1.014	5.242	.902	5.268	.961	5.428	.886	5.287	.847	1.149	.333
Feedbsup	4.013	1.519	4.071	1.505	4.044	1.411	4.195	1.439	4.101	1.421	4.102	1.489	.149	.980
Knwldres	4.497	1.039	4.616	1.077	4.643	.903	4.732	.962	4.765	.928	4.694	.956	.469	.800
Motpotin	188.450	65.222	200.315	65.584	198.518	58.753	204.454	61.524	200.432	63.001	193.759	55.571	.458	.808
Socndstr	4.632	.960	4.551	.962	4.429	1.009	4.386	1.058	4.663	.988	4.561	.944	.948	.450
Socsatis	5.635	.757	5.804	.763	5.848	.652	5.909	.735	5.798	.835	5.943	.674	1.012	.410
Supsatis	4.780	1.367	5.013	1.442	4.803	1.472	4.956	1.536	4.949	1.406	5.015	1.279	.368	.871

Table VII.8   Summary of Significance Levels

Variable	Sex	Marital Status	Age	Education	Experience
Skillvar	.501	.040*	.234	.000*	.358
Taskiden	.635	.126	.166	.091	.214
Tasksign	.154	.527	.113	.158	.478
Exmeangf	.953	.839	.165	.195	.429
Autonomy	.691	.791	.849	.168	.636
Exprespn	.691	.791	.849	.168	.636
Gensatis	.982	.156	.115	.253	.555
Ingrnest	.035*	.051	.159	.064	.704
Feedbjob	.966	.191	.065	.051	.333
Feedbsup	.485	.086	.173	.622	.980
Knwldres	.618	.519	.041*	.354	.800
Motpotin	.778	.373	.052	.367	.808
Socndstr	.000*	.588	.721	.052	.450
Socsatis	.204	.388	.010*	.243	.410
Supsatis	.924	.807	.264	.851	.871

*p value < .05.

CASES AND INCIDENTS FOR WORKSHOPS

About the Contributing Authors

Dr. John E. Dittrich is an Associate Professor of Business Policy in the Graduate School of Business Administration at the University of Colorado. He received his Ph.D. from the University of Washington in Administrative Theory and Organizational Behavior. He has an M.B.A. from Harvard and a B.S. in Industrial Relations from Purdue. After a series of management positions in industry, his final position before pursuing a teaching career was Manager of Administrative Services for the H&D Container Division of Westvaco Corporation. He has written numerous books and articles about equity theory, management development, dimensions of organizational fairness, group decision making, and the personnel management functions.

Dr. Charles L. Hinkle is a Professor of Business Administration in the Graduate School of Business Administration at the University of Colorado. He has a doctorate from Harvard in Business Administration. He received his M.S. degree in Economics from Baylor and his B.S. from the same university. He is also Dean of the School of Bank Marketing, Bank Marketing Association. He has worked extensively in both private and public organizations and has experience in marketing, financial and general management, broadcasting, computer operations, and banking, and has served on boards of directors. In 1975 he was honored as the first recipient of the annual University of Colorado Chancellor's Award for teaching, research and community service. In 1979 he was noted by the faculty and Regents to receive the University of Colorado Medal—their highest award.

The President's Pet Project*

Charles Jacoby, Manager of Systems Analysis and Design for the company's centralized computer operation, was excited and more than a bit apprehensive. The company's president, Wilson Wyatt, had directed Charles to develop a simulation model for use in the Corporate Planning Department and for strategy formulation by the executive committee and the board of directors. Wyatt's comments were explicit. "With the extent of change—inflation—curtailment of supplies, increasing lack of reliability of suppliers, and intensification of competition, our planners and strategists need to have the ability to develop a series of commercial scenarios—each with variables adjusted to reflect changes anticipated in major elements affecting both sales and operations. We need to anticipate crises before they occur—whether they become evident in manpower, financing, raw materials, or in the marketplace."

In thinking over the president's remarks, Charles considered the effect of the new directive on his current project load. Although the existing 360/370 systems had been installed for over six years in some cases, additional applications were backlogged extensively (approximately two years work if all projects were undertaken). In addition, several routine tasks were in need of attention. Systems review and maintenance work had recently been split out of Charles' department and assigned to a new Operations Systems Maintenance Group. This new section

---

*John E. Dittrich, 1980. This case is intended as a vehicle to stimulate discussion and not to illustrate either correct or incorrect administrative procedures.

had been staffed largely be experienced operations personnel and was only now beginning to undertake project assignments.

The second category of more routine work dealt with documentation of systems already installed. In the conversion process, pressures from top management for completion against time deadlines and the typical cost squeeze on his own department had forced Charles to postpone several documentation steps for major systems elements. During initial installation stages, while minor changes and debugging were underway, and while the system designer was still actively involved, Charles was not overly concerned with documentation. With designs debugged and operating relatively smoothly and with the designers working on other projects (and in some cases working for other companies), Charles was becoming increasingly uneasy. He believed that the documentation work, although certainly much less glamorous than some of the new design projects, was critical to continued operations and essential as the original designers became farther removed from their completed systems work. He therefore had established as a major departmental objective the documentation work on three major subsystems. His boss, Nathan Ellsberg, was in complete agreement and expressed considerable concern over the vulnerability of the computer shop without the needed reference documents. He had told Charles that these three documentation projects were "must items" as far as he was concerned, and they would be a significant element in Charles' personal performance review, due in ten months.

Charles believed that while the staff he had built was extremely competent, they had developed their reputation for competence on the basis of their ability to solve complex problems. Several had achieved regional and national prominence for papers presented in professional meetings. Many had received (and rejected) offers from computer system design shops in other companies, some at much higher salary levels. A brief summary of Charles' key staff members' qualifications follows.

Albert Janeway   Age 26. B.S. Purdue (Honors) in computer science. Hired as systems analyst trainee at 22, served as junior analyst on executive program development for remote terminal applications. Currently project leader. Excellent programmer. Systems design work has been both innovative and cost effective. Frequently works weekends and evenings.

Sandy Ebersole   Age 29. B.A. Smith College; M.B.A. Harvard. Hired at age 26 as systems design trainee, has served as programmer, junior designer, and now project leader on medium-sized projects. Excellent analyst. First-class business sense. Particularly well suited to cost analysis of current and anticipated systems. Outspoken, hardworking.

Douglas Dickey   Age 40. B.B.A. (Accounting) Indiana University; (Systems Emphasis) Ohio State University. CPA. Hired at age 36 as systems analyst. Served as CPA and systems designer for one of the "big eight" accounting firms for eight years. Exceptional on accounting and financial security systems projects. Works better as senior analyst than team leader.

Karl Kaufman   Age 38. B.S.M.E. Carnegie Tech; M.S. (Computer Science) Purdue. Hired as operations systems specialist at age 35. Work experience as engineer and systems designer for production departments of several major companies, including one competitor. Specializes in management control systems. A perfectionist. Works most Saturdays, and usually until 6 p.m. each evening. Has presented papers at regional and national professional meetings. Regarded as a national expert in operational management systems.

Bob Bateman   Age 32. B.B.A. (Marketing) University of Wisconsin. Eight years of employment experience with a competitor in market research and data analysis. Has attended vendor seminars on computer applications in marketing and market research. Familiar with FORTRAN, COBOL, and some machine languages. National reputation for use of computer systems in market analysis and forecasting demand patterns.

Cecilia Knopf   Age 27. B.S. with honors (Computer Science) University of Colorado. Employed at age 23 as programmer/analyst trainee. Experienced in FORTRAN, COBOL, and software development. Employed during college by software development firm. Excellent recommendations. Performance exceptionally strong on internal control and execution routines for the CPU and disk I/O units. Currently senior systems analyst. Occasionally serves as team leader on smaller projects.

In considering the major tasks for the year, Charles was impressed by the need to perform well in both. The president's project had high visibility and support. Further, it would entail the challenges of advanced design, and would be an extremely stimulating project to work on. The documentation work—regarded as essential by both Charles and Nathan—was a "housekeeping" project of little concern to laymen, but badly needed to secure and maintain the development of the company's systems.

Why Tinker With It?*

Ed Jarvis was puzzled by recent events. As newly appointed Manager of System Operations Maintenance of the company's centralized computer center, he and most of his senior staff had seen the center grow enormously. From a punchcard machine accounting shop used to maintain financial accounting records the center had expanded to be a complex incorporating an IBM 3033, several disk I/O units, tape drives for monthly and weekly payroll and accounting routines, high-speed printing capacity, and several remote terminals.

For Ed, the growth had been both challenging and rewarding. Much of the systems design work on the various expansion stages had been done by a project team made up of vendor analysts and company systems analysts and programmers assigned from the Systems Analysis Section, headed by Charles Jacoby, an M.S. (Computer Science) graduate of Carnegie-Mellon, hired about 5 years earlier. Both Ed and Charles reported to Nathan Ellsberg, Vice President of Administrative Operations. Although Ed hadn't been directly involved in design work, he had been called on to assist in systems review meetings and in the planning and implementation of changes as they occurred. His staff had been selected from operations personnel. All had progressed through each of the stages of transition—learning new routines, taking courses offered by vendors, and seeing their jobs altered as hardware and systems changes were made.

---

*John E. Dittrich, 1980. This case is intended as a vehicle to stimulate discussion and not to illustrate either correct or incorrect administrative procedures.

Recently, as a part of his system maintenance activities, Ed had been asked to undertake a review and redesign of the systems used to handle sales and billing transactions. The systems in question had been in use for over six years, and seemed overdue for reexamination and modification. The project sounded interesting to Ed—and somewhat at variance with his group's normal assignments. When he asked if he would be able to get help from Charles' programmers and analysts, he learned that they were all engaged in a major project dealing with comprehensive sales/operations forecasting for the corporate planning department, a project given A-1 priority by the president of the company.

Ed reviewed the project with his senior staff and was surprised at their lack of interest. Pete Zifferelli, formerly manager of data control, seemed to exemplify the staff's response when he said, "Hell, Ed, that system's fine— why tinker with it? We haven't had any significant error costs associated with that system since it was debugged over six years ago." Ed had little to rejoin with except a comment to the effect that old systems, while useful, may lack service features that newer systems might have, and may be less efficient with respect to service time and space utilization.

Ed's key staff, and a brief outline of their backgrounds, are as follows.

Gregory Olson   Age 43. B.B.A. University of California at Fullerton. Employed as accounting clerk at age 27, machine accountant at 32, shift supervisor machine accounting at age 34, most recently shift supervisor of computer room operations. Has had FORTRAN and COBOL programming courses.

Sally Everson   Age 36. High school plus a two-year certification in bookkeeping from Valley Community College.

Hired as keypunch operator at age 25, senior keypunch operator at 28, supervisor of data entry at 30, most recently shift supervisor of data entry and control. No programming or systems design experience or training.

Edgar Astrala Age 53. High school plus two years accounting at Bear Creek Vocational Center. Employed at age 27 as bookkeeper. Machine accountant trainee at age 34, machine accountant at 35, shift supervisor of machine accounting at age 41, has been shift supervisor of computer operations since age 44. No programming or systems design training.

Pete Zifferelli Age 42. B.B.A. University of Akron, M.B.A. Wayne State University. First employed as cost analyst at age 29, senior cost analyst and team leader at age 32, assigned to computer development and installation team at age 34, and data control supervisor at age 37. Has had training in both FORTRAN and COBOL, and participated in system design work during the conversion process.

As Ed made a mental review of his senior staff's qualifications, he considered the problem. A nine-month deadline had been tentatively set for the review and redesign project. Some additional funding might be available to cover travel and other miscellaneous costs, but Ed's group was expected to perform the revision project concurrently with their normal activities.

Consolidated Fidelity—Implementing Change*

In preparing its "Progress and Profits for the Eighties" campaign, Consolidated Fidelity Insurance Corporation was considering ways to improve planning, implementation, and control mechanisms at the home office and in regional offices that served the fifty states, Puerto Rico, and the Virgin Islands. A recent issue of the company employee magazine printed excerpts of a speech by CF's president Stephen Wallace, who expressed "dismay at the unsettling seventies" but affirmed that he was "quite optimistic about the eighties and that Consolidated will capitalize on the decade's myriad opportunities." Wallace cited social, political, and economic problems that would continue to test managers' mettle and said he was confident that most of the company's employees would improve productivity, become more dedicated than ever before to corporate goals, and find deep satisfaction in their jobs. At a recent management conference, the president had asked top officers to think creatively about ways to improve "profit performance and people development. In the eighties," he said, "we must learn to deal more effectively with our employees, to motivate them toward achieving CF's objectives; this means improving our humanagement skills to get more team effort and overall loyalty. By 'humanagement' I mean management that is humanistic—helping our employees learn how to make maximum contributions to Consolidated. In turn, the or-

---

*Charles Hinkle, 1980. This case is intended as a vehicle to stimulate discussion and not to illustrate either correct or incorrect administrative procedures.

ganization must offer people adequate incomes and job security."

The company had a process for reviewing and appraising employees' job performance, but had not attempted to get various divisions, departments, and work areas involved in an overall, integrated planning effort. The president and numerous managers, particularly those in the regions and several at the home office, had expressed interest in MBO; a few field managers practiced joint goalsetting in developing sales goals, and an operations group supervisor in data processing was applying this technique in her area. Many managers at CF had been exposed to MBO, planning and leadership concepts at periodic company training sessions.

Margaret Shane, age 26, a Smith graduate in mathematics, had three years of experience in developing computer programs for CF's commercial underwriting division and three years as a project leader and unit manager before accepting the recent assignment as assistant to the soon-to-retire director of personnel.

Shane believed that along with regular management training programs, goalsetting processes should be set up so the company could have more specific directions at the lowest levels and some means of measuring productivity. She got approval from her boss to explore these notions with others at the home office, which was all the encouragement Shane needed to develop a notebook of materials for putting such an effort into practice. The notebook contained trade periodical articles lauding MBO, examples of how the idea had worked in other institutions, and a set of forms for managers to use in implementing MBO. A copy of the notebook was sent to key managers at headquarters and at regional offices.

Several managers and first-line supervisors expressed to Shane their support, saying they were enthusiastic about the possibilities, and a few agreed to help her sell the idea in the company. Her boss commented favorably and suggested that she try to build a base of support at the home office, then draft a proposal for installing such a planning system. "I know you can persuade some of the hardheads around here that MBO can work, that it's not just a buzzword or a passing fad. All these youngsters we're hiring—this could be just what's needed to get them into the real world of hard work and accomplishment."

"Margaret," a former DP co-worker remarked, "I can understand why you want to do this—it would help the company, that's for sure. And it would be a feather in your cap at the same time. But, believe me, you need help and I don't think you're going to find anybody here who's experienced and has the time to work with you. Why don't you get some outside help?" Shane remembered a seminar on leadership styles in which Claiborne Haverhill, a management consultant, had briefly discussed the promises and pitfalls of goalsetting and planning. She called him, made an appointment for the following week, and mailed him the MBO notebook. In the conversation, she learned that he had been involved in developing CF's employee handbook and was somewhat familiar with the organization.

Claiborne Haverhill, 45 years of age, had an M.B.A. from City College, New York, and a Ph.D. in industrial psychology from Boston University. After he and Shane had discussed various aspects of planning and goalsetting, Haverhill suggested that the first step should be to conduct a job diagnostic survey, using a questionnaire and personal interviews, in departments in which the contemplated changes might be introduced. Over lunch, Shane and Haverhill discussed their ideas with four area supervisors and two assistant vice presidents from DP. "Before we break up," the consultant said, "a suggestion. I believe that the ideal procedure would be to have one of the larger departments implement the full-fledged MBO program and another department of comparable size do nothing, serving as the control group in an experiment. Then motivation, performance, satisfaction, and absenteeism would be evaluated between the two groups. If MBO works, it can safely be installed throughout the organization." Consideration was given to working first with the programmer/ analyst and operations groups in the company's DP division.

Neither of the DP assistant vice presidents was willing to serve as the control group because, as one of them put it, "We already have enough problems without being guinea pigs. My people wouldn't stand for it, I'm afraid. Morale is already pretty low." The speaker had a reputation for getting things done. He had started at Consolidated as a programming trainee, and later worked a year in operations before leaving to work at another insurance company where he was employed for three years before returning to CF in 1974. He was a strong advocate of in-house technical management courses but because of the many daily crises that required his presence could seldom find time to attend.

The other assistant vice president at the luncheon, who was in his late thirties, had been with CF since his discharge from the U.S. Marines in 1968. "My people already have plenty to do," he said, "a helluva lot more than they can handle. I'm already pressing them to the wall on deadlines. I think these are OK ideas, but I'm not gung-ho on starting something new right now. Why don't we wait until things settle down a bit and the workload is under control?"

Shane knew that her boss would be unhappy with no action at all and she felt that the company's president would be displeased unless personnel took the lead in organizing an attempt at MBO. To herself, she mused, "Why doesn't the president just send out a directive?" Then she offered this suggestion: "Mr. Haverhill, could you attend our regular management session tomorrow and give some of the key points about MBO and how it might work at Consolidated?" The consultant agreed to be there at two o'clock.

At the Friday afternoon meeting, Haverhill reviewed the pluses and minuses of the system he had in mind, emphasized the need for "setting priorities, establishing specific targets, and following up to measure results at preestablished intervals." His presentation took an hour, concluding with the admonition that Consolidated would be well advised to conduct an employee attitude survey before launching an MBO effort. "Also," he said, "participation is the key—the old autocratic approach is outmoded. Democractic leadership—that's what the new-breed employee wants."

A corporate accounting vice president shook the presenter's hand, thanked him, then turned to the audience and concluded, "This has certainly been a helpful presentation from Mr. Haverhill, one that I know will give all of us a lot to think about. Thanks again, Mr. Haverhill. If our president, Mr. Wallace, were here, I'm sure he would be enthusiastic about the idea of getting our management involved in better planning techniques."

Ordinarily the president and the director of personnel attended the biweekly meetings, but neither could attend this particular session because of other appointments—the president was at a reception for a delegation of foreign visitors to the city, and the director of personnel was at an affirmative action conference in Washington, D.C. Several other high-level officers were absent during the first part of the meeting, but some arrived during the last few minutes of Haverhill's comments. One of them commented to another, "I think we ought to get something like MBO going at the company, but I've already been given my goals for the year: my neck's going to be in the noose unless I can cut underwriting losses and improve the low-hazard business." His companion nodded and said, "I'm on the line to reduce expenses by simplifying work. And our automation efforts are dragging." A third joined in, "If I can just expand our prevention publicity and jack up sales and profits, the rest of my problems will take care of themselves. Planning just takes a lot of time that I don't have right now."

The accounting vice president then asked for the group's attention and advised them, "Refreshments have just been delivered, so let's take a quick break before tackling the next item on this afternoon's agenda."

Analyze the situation.

1   Is Consolidated ready for joint goalsetting?

2   Your group has been asked to collaborate with the president, the director of personnel, and his assistant. What advice would you give them, assuming that each is interested in establishing a joint goalsetting at CF?

3   Outline a procedure for implementing joint goalsetting at the company. In your opinion, how could structure and process be established?

Joint Goalsetting Interaction*

Task: Manager and employee in joint goalsetting session.

Setting: Data Processing Department.

Company Background

The company pays salaries above the local average. Annual overall turnover in DP of 28 percent, up from 24 percent two years ago. Turnover in programming/analysis increased to 30 percent the past year, from 26 percent two years previously. Considerable shifting between companies and between departments within the firm.

Several hundred persons employed in the company's headquarters DP group, which comprises analysis, programming, information systems, operations, and a spectrum of state-of-the-art hardware and proprietary software. Numerous successes, yet during the past three years there are indications that the organization as a whole has grown increasingly complacent; some DP units are drifting, resting on their laurels, their members apathetic, interdepartmental frictions seem to be sapping vitality and destroying team spirit. DP absenteeism is up, particularly in programming/analysis, occurring mostly on Mondays and Fridays.

Requests for transfer into your area have been declining of late, despite the unit's excellent reputation for

---

*Charles L. Hinkle, 1980.

development, including significant advances in data compression techniques for on-line business files.

After extensive participation and planning by many, at all levels of management in the structure, the company is inaugurating an MBO plan, a joint goalsetting program. Along with two other departments, DP, often the focal point for important corporate changes, has been selected by the president to introduce the joint goalsetting process. Most DP managers and supervisors are excited about the idea and believe that the cyclical nature of many major DP projects makes them likely candidates for MBO approaches.

After reading the above company background, you will be asked to role play one of the three attached scenarios.

Manager

You have some eight years in DP, five with the present company, experience in programming, operations, and systems analysis. Leader of one major and several minor system development projects. Recently promoted to current job as manager responsible for 25 employees, you have continued to be directly and intensively involved in technical aspects of certain projects in your area of responsibility.

Last year you married a co-worker in DP; it is your second marriage. Your spouse is in a management position in another work area in DP. Spare time is spent with the children. On a typical weekend, both of you will work several hours, usually Saturday, at the office, then pick up the children and visit relatives in a nearby town or engage in some other family-oriented activity. All of you are active in the local Catholic church and take part in children's team athletics, Campfire Girls, and Boy Scouts.

You and your spouse became acquainted while attending night classes at the local college to complete work on an undergraduate degree in computer science.

For the most part, those in your work area are in their late twenties and early thirties. Many are college graduates, principally in liberal arts, a few in computer science or management information systems. Some have associate degrees in DP from the local community college.

You are to meet shortly with employees in your work area to discuss goals for the next several months. You consider yourself to be achievement-oriented and try to practice participative management when appropriate and when you are not too rushed. You feel that the area you are responsible for is characterized by high-scope tasks and that the group members generally have high growth needs.

Last week you held one meeting with the group to announce the MBO program. There were several questions, a few expressions of concern that this could require frequent meetings, and some bantering about updating resumes and visiting local employment agencies. Some, primarily those who had participated in some form of goalsetting procedures at other firms, said they thought that such a framework might provide an orderly way to anticipate and solve difficult problems. There appears to be a climate of mutual trust in the group.

Employee

Scenario One

You are 29, married six years, have two children ages two and four, enjoy gourmet cooking and stamp collecting. You and your spouse also backpack with a wilderness group. Along with co-workers you consider your work area to be a satisfying place to work as well as a springboard for promotion. You think that you have strong creativity and achievement needs and believe that you would even be willing to sacrifice money and job security to fulfill those needs.

You earned an associate degree in DP from the local community college before joining the company two years ago. Previous job experience included service as a cryptographer in the Army and a job as bookkeeper at a nearby manufacturing firm.

Transferring from another work unit in the company, you have been in this area just over six months. Lately you have experienced some difficulty meeting deadlines. To some extent, you suspect, the quality of your work has deteriorated. Also, you have had occasional unpleasant verbal interchanges with co-workers who chided you about arriving late to work, especially on mornings when project team meetings were scheduled. Just this morning you also had words with a user who came in to complain about the layout of a report that you have designed. Twice in the past month you have been absent from the office, feeling "below par." Some marital conflicts have occurred the past few weeks over family financies. Although you ordinarily enjoy your work, you have the gnawing suspicion that your project leader has recently begun assigning you to somewhat trivial jobs.

You are about to meet with your area manager to discuss goals for the next several months. Apart from casual conversation when the manager would appear unannounced at project team meetings, this will be the first private interchange for the two of you. You are interested in finding out the manager's opinion of how well you are doing, not just how well the current project is coming along, and you think it might be appropriate to mention that you have an interest in being appointed project leader of some future task group. You realize the central purpose of the meeting is to discuss goals, but you are not quite sure what MBO is about, and you did miss last week's meeting on this subject.

Scenario Two

After 18 months in the group, your peers have just voted you as "Achiever of the Year," recognition for your on-the-job accomplishments that gives you a great deal of satisfaction. You are proud of your troubleshooting skills and believe that you are an able team leader. The new manager wrote and delivered a letter of commendation on your award, and you received a handwritten note of congratulations from the DP vice president. You have assumed a social leadership position in your work area, enjoy having coffee and chit-chat with co-workers and people from other groups. Occasionally you have wine-tasting parties at your apartment, events always well attended by people from DP and other departments in the company. You are usually one of the first to appear at the Friday Afternoon Club and are often the center of attention, telling stories about your experience in the Peace Corps. You are considered to be a sharp dresser and a good dancer.

"If the truth were known," you remarked to your roommate one evening recently, "I have a great deal more potential than is being utilized at work. True, I like my job, but there are other challenges I'd like to tackle." It has crossed your mind to make it known that you'd like to try for the next DP manager's job that opens up, but are not sure that you have enough "time in grade" on your current assignment. One matter concerns you—lately you seem to have had difficulty making deadlines, especially when working on team efforts, but usually it has been easy for you to cajole others into overlooking these occurrences. Also, there has been moderate criticism for your taking off from work early on occasions to take part in your social work volunteer service at the city mental health clinic, and a few people look askance at your active participation in the county's drug crisis center.

You are slightly ambivalent about the forthcoming goalsetting discussion, but realize that it might provide an opportunity to work with the manager in charting a course to advance your professional interests. The ambivalence comes from your aversion to anyone's looking over your shoulder, and your innate skepticism about management "tools," that the "tool" might be the individual who is to be manipulated by such devices as MBO. But you are resolved to have an open mind on the subject. Your apprehension is offset to an extent by your belief that the manager is a fair person.

The Deficient Programmer Job

Job Title: Business Applications Programmer.

Primary function: Review assigned business problems and attendant documentation such as logic diagrams, and prepare computer programs to accomplish specified solutions.

Reports to: Business Applications Programming Supervisor.

Responsibilities:

1 Under direct supervision, review detailed specifications and develop computing equipment solutions.

2 Analyze logic diagrams and write computer programs that satisfy requirements.

3 Prepare detailed documentation for computer programs, with limited assistance from more experienced programmers and using the "Programming Standards and Techniques" manual as a guide.

4 Verify the logic of computer programs by using developed test data in trial runs.

5 With the assistance of more experienced programmers, debug developed computer programs to ensure proper operation during production runs.

6 Assist in preparing detailed instructions for the Computer Operator's use during production runs.

7 Assist in determining causes of computer operation malfunctions.

8 Under direct supervision, apply improved solutions to programming problems.

9 Devote constant effort toward acquiring and maintaining a working knowledge of higher-level programming languages such as COBOL, FORTRAN, and PL/1; use all available educational sources.

Please complete the following evaluation of this workshop. We are very interested in your comments and encourage you to take the time to share your analysis of the session.

Topic: _____   **Presenter:** _____

1. Value of this session:

        _____   _____   _____   _____   _____

        Extremely   Very   Average   Very   Worthless
          Valuable   Good   Poor

2. What did you like most about the workshop?

3. What can we do to make this workshop more meaningful?

4. Rate the presenter(s):

        Excellent ____ ____ ____ ____ ____ ____ Poor

                        Average

5. Comment about the presenter(s):

6. Other comments:

Please complete the following evaluation of this session. We are very interested in your comments and encourage you to take the time to share your analysis of the session.

Topic: _____ **Presenter:** _____

1. Value of this session:

Extremely Valuable	Very Good	Average	Very Poor	Worthless

2. What did you like most about the session?

3. What did you like least about the session?

4. Rate the presenter(s):

Excellent ____ ____ ____ ____ ____ ____ Poor

Average

5. Comment about the presenter(s):

6. Other Comments:

Please complete the following evaluation of this workshop. We are very interested in your comments and encourage you to take the time to share your analysis of the session.

_____

Topic: _____**Presenter:** _____

1. Value of this session:

    _____   ____   _____   ____   _____
    Extremely   Very   Average   Very   Worthless
    Valuable   Good   Poor

2. What did you like most about the workshop?

3. What can we do to make this workshop more meaningful?

4. Rate the presenter(s):

    Excellent ____ ____ ____ ____ ____ ____ Poor
                            Average

5. Comment about the presenter(s):

6. Other comments:

INDEX

211

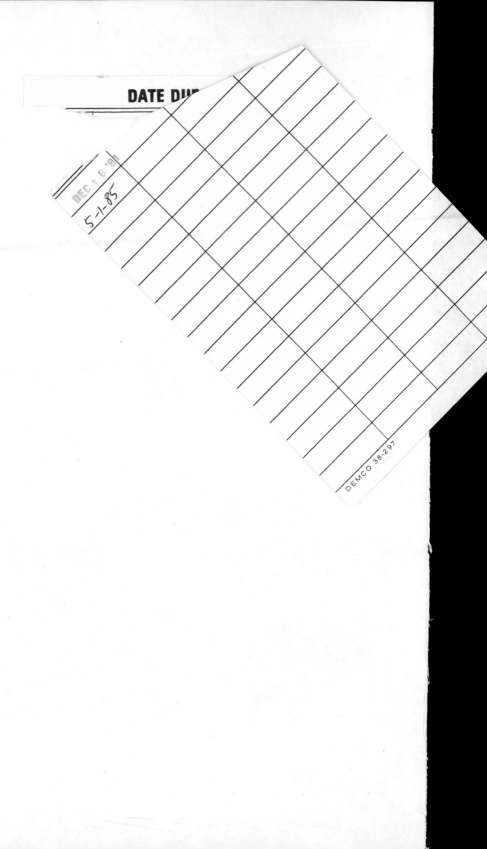

DEMCO 38-297